Go or Don't Go has a profound message for entrepreneurs, business owners and career professionals: the secrets to success are within you and the steps are easy to apply if you follow her brilliant "Money Acceleration" template that has helped thousands of people achieve their financial dreams. It's also very personal and sweet: the author shares her own struggles as she shows you how to manifest your own story of success happen. I highly recommend this book to everyone…and I love some of the brain-based strategies she's included, like yawning! Bravo!

—*Mark Waldman, Executive MBA Faculty,*
College of Business, Loyola Marymount University

Layer by layer, Kate has stuck with me and given me tools that help me remain in the 5 percent of those who are able to keep their businesses open after five years. Not only have I remained open, but I have expanded.

—*Nicky Stansbury, Owner, NichoLyn Coaching*

Revenue is up more than 50 percent, and I am on track to achieve the work/life balance I have been striving for. I recommend working with Kate to everyone I know who is looking to get unstuck in their business FAST!

—*Leise Jones, Owner, Leise Jones Photography*

I was stuck with pricing, finding my focus, and growing my business. Kate will produce quick results, and the community she fosters is incredible. I highly recommend Kate to anyone who wants to enjoy being an entrepreneur.

—*Brandy Sales, Video Expert and Coach*

What a gift to find a coach who has extensive knowledge in the business world and is an expert tapping coach. If you're looking to grow your business, then Kate is the coach for you.

—*Jessica Ortner, Founder and Producer, The Tapping Solution*

By the end of the nine-month program with Kate, I went from being unemployed to billing for $8,000. Kate's blend of working with mental beliefs, attitudes, and blocks, as well as the practical tips combined with her gentle yet firm pushing to take action has been ideal for my style. And then there's the great support and cheerleading for steps taken. My confidence and vision for my business have grown exponentially.

—*Kathleen Hennessy, Owner, PeaceWorks Coaching*

Kate is very good, quick, and efficient. Her work is very much about be, do, have. Expect massive energy shifts and major breakthroughs. To quote Mastercard, the results are "priceless."

—*Andrew Joy, Owner, The JoyKey*

I was not doing as well as I knew was possible while I was struggling on my own. I had tried other systems and failed and was a little scared to try again. Now that I have seen the power of working with Kate, I am more sure of everything and would recommend Kate to anyone. Her work is an art and it is brilliant. Thank you, Kate Beeders!!!

—*Colleen Sonmor, www.myinnerbeautyspa.com*

After some gentle (and some not-so-gentle) nudging to raise my rates, which I had not done in a few years, I finally did so—practically doubling them. This definitely challenged some beliefs I was holding onto, including the fear that no one would pay that much. Within a few hours of tapping with Kate, I booked my first client at the new rate. As I don't believe in coincidences, I'm inclined to call Kate Beeders a miracle worker. Thank you, Kate!

—*Brad Yates, Coach*

I'm so excited to share that I manifested my trip to Italy. Using Kate's systems brought me the exact amount I needed for my dream vacation with my husband. Thank you, Kate!

—*Gina Noel Decker, www.techdoneforyou.com*

For more celebrations, visit www.KateBeeders.com/success.

Go or Don't Go

The Complete Guide to Accelerate Your Success and Tap into Your Brilliance

KATE BEEDERS

Go or Don't Go
First Edition, 2018

Copyright © 2018 by Kate M. Beeders

Published by:
Kate M. Beeders
Boston, Massachusetts
www.KateBeeders.com

Paperback: 978-1-7321003-0-5
Ebook: 978-1-7321003-1-2

Printed in the United States of America
10 9 8 7 6 5 4 3 2 1

If I am not for myself, who will be for me?
If I am not for others, what am I?
And if not now, when?
—RABBI HILLEL

Having the honor of holding my Dad's hand as he took his final breaths made me realize this was my "Go or Don't Go" moment. This experience—his life, my life—needed to mean something, no more holding back and not sharing my valuable message with more people. It was time for me to show up even more in my brilliance. It was critical this book came to life.

The two people who influenced me the most in my life are my parents. This book is dedicated to both of them.

This book is in honor of my Dad, Dr. Herbert Beeders, who didn't have many material goods growing up, yet walked to school a zillion miles each day to realize his dream of becoming a dentist. He taught me about preventive care and how it can improve the shape and quality of my life. His belief that things always work out has provided inner strength for me. He was a very special man.

My Mom, Sylvia Beeders, taught my siblings and me about determination and inner strength. Her motto has always been: "You don't ask, you don't get." These characteristics have been a constant source of inspiration throughout my journey. If you notice a bit of dry humor in this book, that's "the Beeders sense of humor," as my Mom says. "It's like the abominable snowman. There are traces of it but you're never quite sure if it exists."

Contents

Introduction: Tapping to Success

It seems unbelievable that only a few short years ago, I was a dead-broke waitress, dealing with painful carpal tunnel syndrome because I lost my fabulous high-six-figure job when the economy tanked. I had given up hoping that my boyfriend would ride up on his white horse and rescue me. Now, here I am in Hollywood, in my stylish sequined dress, receiving a best-selling author award in the same hotel where the Oscars were once held. And these days, my coach likes to remind me that I'm a member of the exclusive 5 percent club, which is made up of entrepreneurs who earn well over six figures and have a profitable business. Amazing how things can change!

DECISIONS, DECISIONS

When I was working in the corporate world, I was a business development executive, making a lot of money, which allowed me to live a fabulous lifestyle. I took many vacations each year and had lots of expendable income. That was before the economy crashed.

A concern that played over and over in my head after losing my job was: Is it possible to have both a career and lifestyle I love—or must I choose between one or the other? Part of my personal mission was to uncover an answer.

I didn't set out to be an entrepreneur. I did it quite accidentally. I fell in love with a mindset technique called "tapping," achieved many high-level certifications in it, and started trying it on other people. I knew I wanted something different, something better. And my heart wasn't in accepting any of the job offers I had received.

Not really knowing what I was doing in the beginning, I used my business development background to build my client list. In my past career, I used the same techniques to build a list of many multimillion-dollar clients. In the process, being an introvert, I had to learn what my marketing message was, as well as how to initiate sales conversations, overcome objections, and discover the magic price point, all while maintaining client relationships for over 16 years and getting prized referrals. As it turns out, these were the same skills needed for a successful entrepreneurial business.

WHAT'S MY SECRET?

When other entrepreneurs observed how many clients I was attracting so quickly in my business, they wanted to know how I did it. What was my secret? Hence, my coaching business found its niche and direction. Little did they know, in those early days, I was doing trades, offering discounts, and giving away my services. In fact, when I started, my income was embarrassingly low. That was a big area I mastered and what led me to teaching "Charging What You're Worth," as there is no point in having a business without making money.

I hired two great mentors, one for business development and the other for mindset (since no one at the time had the high expertise in both that I required). With their help, I was able to accelerate my income to six figures in the beginning of year two, and it has continued to grow each year.

Over the first two years of my business, I tried many strategies and techniques. Some worked better than others. Those experiments resulted in developing my Money Acceleration System™, which I have used with entrepreneurial and professional clients all over the world to help them break through to the next level.

WHAT A DIFFERENCE A FEW YEARS MAKES

Not only have I achieved all this success very quickly, but I also have been invited to be a keynote speaker all over North America, be interviewed in telesummits with over 500,000 listeners worldwide, and host international retreats. The first book I wrote, *The Winning Way*, was an international best-seller. And for several years, I hosted a widely popular radio show, "Tapping to Success," on which the upper-echelon leaders in motivation, transformation and business coaching were frequent guests.

I share my story with you not from a place of ego, but to tell you that if I can do this, so can you. In some ways, it was easier than I thought, and in many other ways, it was much harder than I could have ever expected.

For example, any investment I made in my business, I needed to earn money to pay for it. I didn't have anyone to pay my bills, a trust fund, inheritance, or a sugar daddy. I did it all on my own and found a way to make my success happen.

RUNNING OUT OF OPTIONS

The system that I will be teaching you in this book has helped thousands worldwide, including one of my longtime clients, who, when we first started working together, told me quite clearly, "This has to work." She was out of other options. Five years later, her income is well over six figures, she has multiple locations, and she has built a thriving business.

The Money Acceleration System™ has also helped another of my clients, Andrea, who at almost 60 years old was laid off from her lifelong job. At that age, she felt she wasn't hirable and didn't know what else to do but start her own business. Her idea for her niche was terrific. However, the problem was she didn't know how to make money or get clients. Andrea felt desperate—she needed this venture to work and was at her wit's end. She was excited enough about what she wanted to create that she borrowed money from a friend to pay for coaching services with me. When we met, she was unemployed and had zero income.

Working with me was a massive leap of faith for Andrea. But the investment paid off. Not only did her income rise from zero to $8,000 a month, but she was also able to travel, save money, and pay her friend back. Andrea accomplished this success in less than nine months, because she wanted this to happen and she followed all my steps to the letter.

IT'S YOUR TURN

In this book, you will learn how to create, set, and reach your goals. I'm going to teach you how to give yourself permission to dream big. On the flip side, you will be learning how to overcome the fears, doubt, beliefs, and old stories that hold you back.

We're going to take this step by step, so this time you finally achieve your success. I'll be as transparent as possible, sharing my stories as well as those of my clients, which I hope will inspire you to tap into your brilliance.

Whenever I teach, I set three very powerful intentions for my students:

1. To teach you the content you came for
2. To open the doors of possibilities to what you are capable of and what you deserve
3. To bring you into a broader community of like-minded people

Before we get too much further, I recommend you purchase a journal to complete the exercises in this book and jot down the valuable takeaways. I love using journals when I am learning and transforming.

One of my clients was so excited about my concept that when she signed up to work with me, she kept repeating that she was ready to be brilliant. Now, it's your turn.

BREAK THROUGH TO YOUR BRILLIANCE

I was a senior flight attendant for seven years after graduating from college. Some people consider that career the ultimate experience in customer service, due to the broad range of personalities you must deal with. Besides greeting passengers and ensuring an enjoyable onboard experience, I was in charge of handling emergencies, which could mean evacuating the plane in 90 seconds. I was responsible for everyone's life on board, as in the more severe situations, the pilots are often incapacitated. I took that responsibility very seriously. Understanding the importance of what I am teaching you and my commitment to your success, I take this teaching equally seriously.

For this to work, you must do the same. Working together is always a partnership. I will share my best content on these pages, but it's up to you to take the action steps I give you. If you get stuck or need additional help, you need to take responsibility and reach out for support.

Whether you're an entrepreneur, would-be entrepreneur, or professional in the corporate world, you will experience a lot of transformations by following my teachings in this book.

HOW THIS BOOK IS ORGANIZED

Each chapter will walk you through the steps of how to break through your glass ceiling. There will be questions, worksheets, and exercises to support you. This is exactly what I have done and what I have taught my clients, which has allowed me to skyrocket my success.

At the end of each chapter, I will recap the key points in the "Lessons In Brilliance" section. In my vast experience, I have seen areas where people get stuck, which is why I created the "Don't Get Hijacked" section to help you continue to move forward.

When I trained to be a flight attendant, we spent a lot of time learning how to deal with a potential hijacking, and we took a lot of precautions. After all, if you're heading to Boston, the last thing you want to happen is for your plane to be unexpectedly diverted to a destination you don't want to go to. Throughout the book, I will be sharing situations where you might get hijacked and get off track.

I'm honored and delighted to be your guide as you break through to your brilliance.

1

The Money Acceleration System™

I believe that people have visions of success, yet no matter how smart they are or how hard they work, most don't achieve their dreams. I believe that most people are blinded by how much brilliance they have, and as a result, they continually play a much smaller game in life.

Entrepreneurship is the fastest-growing industry, especially for women. But most of these people are dreamers. People become entrepreneurs because they're excited and passionate about something, and they think that having one more certification or taking one more type of action is going to change everything. It doesn't.

People in the corporate world are willing to work a zillion hours, trading everything else for this potential success, believing it will change everything. That was me many years ago. It doesn't work.

There's a reason you haven't had all of the success you wanted in the past, and you'll find out why in this book.

COMMITTED, OR MERELY INTERESTED?

You're going to find that in some ways my system is much simpler than you expected, as it will be easier for you to take action and see changes. In other ways, it will be more difficult, as it will require commitment on your side. Commitment to you and your dreams. People who are successful are committed; the others are merely interested and not willing to do what it takes. More about that in the chapters to come.

The formula I developed helped me not only skyrocket my business success past my dreams, but it allowed me to teach my clients how to achieve similar success. For some, it was a place they have been dreaming about for years; for others, they realized a level of success they never even dreamed or knew was possible.

THE MONEY ACCELERATION SYSTEM™

Since I've developed this revolutionary formula, I've used the Money Acceleration System™ repeatedly in my business and life. The reason is, it takes you step by step through the actions and strategies required, as well as where your mindset needs to be. After all, your mindset is at least 90 percent responsible for your success (or failure).

The Money Acceleration System™ consists of five zones, each leading to the next one:

1. Comfort Zone
2. Money Zone
3. Action Zone
4. Freak-out Zone
5. Zone of Brilliance

After reaching your Zone of Brilliance, there will be a time when you decide you want to move to the next level and break through that current glass ceiling. At that point, you will repeat the system again. The formula never stops working for you, unless you stop using it.

NOTHING STAYS THE SAME

There has to be a reason for you to want to change. Either you want something better, or you no longer want to be where you are. We're either growing or dying. We don't stay static. Too often people start to move forward and take actions towards their dreams and then something stops them. When you do this often enough, it starts to make the possibility of reaching your dreams a faint distant memory.

When I was a flight attendant after college, I learned about this critical moment during takeoff when the captain must decide whether the plane takes off or aborts taking off. During this time, the jet is going about 175 miles per hour and there truly is less than a nanosecond to make this decision. If everything looks good on the instrument panel, and the weather and other critical factors check out as well, they take off. It not, they abort the takeoff and the plane goes back to the gate. If the captain decides too late to abort the takeoff, it might not be a pretty picture. As one pilot recently shared with me, if they wait too long, it becomes an "oh, shit" moment.

This critical decision is the Go or Don't Go™ point.

Let's say you're flying to beautiful Boston to see me. Yay, I can't wait to meet you. You board the flight and the captain gives his welcome announcement. He mentions that the weather isn't great outside. Foggy, rainy, and windy conditions will create a bumpy flight. He requests that you stay in your seat until he lets you know it's all clear by turning off the seat belt sign and making that announcement.

GO OR DON'T GO

You settle into your seat, and the plane gets cleared for takeoff. You're rolling down the runway faster and faster at speeds close to 175 miles per hour. What if at that point, the captain yelled, "Stop! I can't see Boston from here"? And because he can't see his destination from his starting point, he gets scared. All he sees is fog, rain, and a lot of wind. He stops the plane and brings it back to the gate. Some of you will be so freaked out, you'll never get on a plane again. Others will try to find another flight to Boston because you really want to see me. And what if the agent says, "I'm sorry, all the flights to Boston are full for the next week"? By that point, you've lost your opportunity to meet me and have an amazing experience. That would be a real shame.

Now, let's paint a different scenario. You're rolling down the runway, and when you hit that critical point, the plane takes off. Up into the air it goes. The captain says, "It's bumpy and foggy outside." In fact, if you look out, you can't see much of anything. But sure enough, in a few minutes, you're up above the clouds and the remainder of the flight is smooth. You get to your destination of Boston, and it was worth the initial lack of visibility. We greet each other with a big hug!

You will face many "Go or Don't Go" decisions in your life. Go or Don't Go—you decide. Consistently, you will be confronted with decisions that are related to you moving forward. Decisions you often have to make in a nanosecond. Go or Don't Go. Are you willing to take that next step and take off? Are you ready to go?

LET'S BEGIN

Right now, you are in your Comfort Zone, and there are many things you like about it (or you wouldn't be staying there). The problem is, there are also things you dislike. For example, you wish you were being paid more money, given more responsibility, and had more interesting work to do. Perhaps you justify staying in the Comfort Zone because you get a regular paycheck, have a daily routine, and know what your boss expects. So, you remain where you are. And you're not happy.

Maybe you're an entrepreneur and you wish you were making more money and had more clients. You convince yourself that you don't have the money to invest in mentorship or the resources needed for your success to happen, so you justify staying where you are. You're not happy. You're meant for much bigger things.

Or perhaps you're like my client Sue. She is a technology business consultant who wanted to get more clients and make more money, and the things she had tried in the past hadn't worked for her. Sue hated sales calls and hated networking. She felt defeated and wondered if anything would ever change. So, she made an internal decision to stop doing things that cost money. Sue remained home, rarely spent any money, and didn't go places.

In fact, she stayed in her pajamas most days. As her income dropped lower, so did her lifestyle, until Sue wasn't doing very many activities. Only because she had heard me interviewed did she decide to take a chance and hire me as her coach. She realized through our work together that she had locked herself in the Comfort Zone. Sue had stopped even allowing herself to dream of something more. We did the hard work of releasing past experiences and beliefs that had led to fears and doubts about her success.

As a result, Sue now gets interview requests for her advanced work in her field and has a waiting list of clients who want to work with her. She takes several vacations a year, sold her home, and moved to a beachfront house.

People stay in their Comfort Zone because it's familiar. In this place, you have an expectation of what the world will give you and how to show up. Think of it as a thermostat. If the temperature is set to 68 degrees, no matter what the weather is outside, the temperature inside will remain at that setting. You're the same way.

For a long time, a neighbor worked in a department store that required she wear all black. Recently, she was laid off from her job and acquired other employment. She still dresses completely in black, even though it's no longer required. I have never even seen her accessorize with another color. Wearing all black is her Comfort Zone.

That's why people who lose weight gain it right back; although they most likely don't like weighing more, that's how they know themselves. If someone who has a lot of credit card debt gets a gift of cash and pays off that balance, they often will go right back to charging more. They're used to being in debt. Sales professionals often find it difficult to increase their earnings, as they hit the same goal year after year, unless they have the proper mentorship to help them break through.

One of my clients, Marie, wanted abundance so desperately, yet every time she was close, she would self-sabotage. Every time she was feeling more prosperous and things were going well in her business, an "emergency" would pop up and bring her back to chaos and drama. She was finally able to make that shift to successful, and in the rest of this book, I'll share many of the types of exercises I did with her to permanently remove her from her Comfort Zone and into her Zone of Brilliance.

ANYTHING IS POSSIBLE

If you're not willing to take that first step, you will forever be trapped in your Comfort Zone. There is a danger of taking up permanent residence there. Some people have the mistaken belief that they can settle there. They tell themselves that things aren't that bad. The truth is that things are always moving and changing. If you aren't keeping up with your dreams and what is going on in the outside world, you will end up playing it very small in the game of life.

There are only two reasons to leave the Comfort Zone. You're either moving to a place of desire and love or running from a place of fear and scarcity.

A MOTHER'S LOVE

In my twenties, I was a smoker who had attempted quitting many times, yet always found it too difficult to give up. Finally, I stopped smoking after recovering from a very serious flu. My Mother had called to check on me when I was sick and heard me puffing in the background (any true smoker knows that you can always smoke no matter how sick you are). She made this remark to me that she couldn't believe how stupid I was to smoke when I was so sick. That did it for me. I was willing to go through withdrawal (which can be horrible and why most people aren't able to quit) because I refused to have anyone think I was stupid.

I admit fear is what propelled me out of the Comfort Zone when I started my business. I decided not to get another job or have a boss, and I didn't want to fail and go back with my tail between my legs. That was such a strong fear that it kept me moving forward into entrepreneurship.

When I decided to host a radio show in the beginning years of my business, with some of the top experts in my industry as guests, I was willing to get out of my Comfort Zone as an introvert because I had a vision of where it would take my business and me. I didn't want to be just another coach. I had a desire to get my name out there and start making a difference. That meant getting uncomfortable and hiring a mentor to help me with my fear of public speaking.

WHAT IS IN YOUR COMFORT ZONE?

First, take a few deep breaths. I recommend trying to tune in and listen to your inner guidance, higher self, The Universe, or if you're religious, God—whatever you use as a trusted source. Listen to that intelligence that exists that is bigger than you. Then, take a few quiet, undisturbed minutes and ask yourself the following questions:

1. Where are the places I am settling in my business or my life?
2. When do I say to myself "why bother" or "it is what it is"?
3. In what situations do I have the belief that things will never change for me?

4. In what situations do I make my decisions based on "shoulds" or what others tell me to do?
5. What would I like to change in my life and business?

Without judgment, read what you just wrote. For now, don't worry about how things will change or what you need to do. We're going to take this step by step. You will get all the answers you need in the chapters to come.

Now, ask yourself four more questions, again taking quiet, undisturbed time:

1. *What is the upside of staying where you are right now?* For a lot of people, the answer to this question is the familiarity of what to expect and of what they know.
2. *What is the downside of staying where you are right now?* Ask yourself about all the areas you feel stuck, struggling, disappointed, and playing a much smaller game than you would like to.
3. *What is the upside of moving to the next level?* What are the cool things that would happen to you? Examples of physical results are vacations, a dream home, opportunities, more money in the bank, what you can do for your family/community, and so on. Emotional results are confidence, power, recognition, freedom, safety, and so on.
4. *What is the downside of you moving to that next level?* A lot of people at first say to me that they don't think there would be a downside. I challenge you on that because there always is. Perhaps you're afraid you would have to work too hard, eliminate boundaries, become overly visible, take something from someone else, risk someone getting mad at you, and so on.

Question number four is often where my clients get stuck. Frequently, I hear from my clients who are planning on raising their pricing that they are afraid current clients will get mad at them. Sometimes, they are scared people will want things from them (e.g., money) if they earn more. Or on the flip side, they are afraid they will lose friends if they become successful.

One of my clients, Michele, was afraid of how her husband would view her new success. She had an opportunity to have the job of her dreams. They had been married for over 20 years, and he had always been the breadwinner. She was concerned that this promotion would mean she would become the top supporter of her family, and she didn't know how her husband would react. Michele resisted and resisted going for the more significant position.

When we started working together, one of the action steps I told her to take was to have a conversation with her husband about this new level. Much to her surprise, he was delighted for her income increase, as that would take some of the financial burdens off him. If she hadn't had this conversation, she would forever be living in her Comfort Zone, rereading an old story that she couldn't be more and needed to be "less than" someone else. What a shame! Michele has had several promotions since we started working together, and she and her husband are both enjoying the good life.

You've just learned the initial step to breaking out of your Comfort Zone. Remember, if you want to move to the next level, grow, break through your glass ceiling, and accelerate your success, you must be willing to take this first step.

Congratulations! Now, let's move into the next zone on your journey to success: the Money Zone.

Lessons in Brilliance

✦ The Money Acceleration System™ is made up of five zones. We are starting with the Comfort Zone, which is where you are right now.

✦ The only way you will achieve growth is by being willing to be uncomfortable and get out of your Comfort Zone.

✦ Answer all the questions in this chapter regarding how you are keeping yourself stuck in your business, career or current situation. Include any "aha's" that you get in your journal.

✦ As much as you might want success, there is always a perceived downside of what you will lose at that next level.

► **Don't Get Hijacked!** Your journey has begun. Throughout this book, there will be times you will be tempted to stop. Halting action is a recurring pattern for you. Part of you will be very resistant and want to stay exactly where you are. That is happening for a reason, and it doesn't need to continue. Keep reading, and you'll uncover the secret. Go!

2

Give Yourself Permission to Dream Big!

You can't hit a target without knowing where you want to go. So many people come to me wanting my help, yet they have no idea of what success would look like for them. They don't know how they want to earn that additional money or what they would do with it. They aren't clear about how their life would be different. Sometimes, they vaguely declare the extra income would help pay off debt or be used for travel. If you don't take the time to get clarity of what the next level looks like, things won't change. For example, you'll stay in debt (by continually buying things you can't afford), or you won't take those vacations to dream destinations.

Often, they'll tell me they want to make six figures because in their mind, that's the magic number. Once they've reached six figures, then they reach for multi-six-figures, and so on. For many, they have to keep going higher and higher, never feeling satisfied. They're on a trajectory to keep up with others, without taking the time to figure out what is best for them.

YOU CAN'T HIT A MOVING TARGET

For you to move forward, three essential stages must happen in the Money Zone: clarity, desire, and belief.

Here's what you need to do first. Decide what your destination is. That starts by creating a powerful vision statement of where you are heading. By taking that first action, you will get clarity of where you are going, allowing you to focus and accelerate your journey.

As a result, you are deliberately creating what you want to happen in your life. Ultimately, this is putting you in charge of your life, instead of the other way around. Being in a place of power is key to your success. More about that later in the book.

As a very young girl, I learned about the power of manifestation. I used to watch reruns of the television show "Bewitched," and I loved Samantha. I wanted to be her when I grew up and thought it was my destiny, since my Uncle Sol had created this show. I walked around the house wiggling my nose, expecting things to magically show up, like they did for Samantha. She'd clean messy rooms instantly and have delicious cakes suddenly appear on the kitchen counter. She made all sorts of amazing things transpire with the wiggle of her nose. That's the kind of life I dreamed of.

Well, fast-forward all these years later, and even though I didn't become Samantha, I learned about the power of manifestation and that there is no limit to what we can have and create in our lives. I've discovered that I'm a very powerful manifester. You can become one, too! All of us deserve to be, do, and have more.

CATCHING YOUR FLIGHT

You'd never go to the airport, go to a random gate, and get on that airplane. Of course not. You'd go to the gate that matches your ticket. Then you'd board the aircraft that will take you to your intended destination. You wouldn't like it if you boarded the plane and the captain announced that instead of going to your planned destination, he thought he would take off and just let the plane go wherever the wind blew it.

If you were heading to Cancun for your dream vacation and instead ended up in Indianapolis, you would be one unhappy camper. (I went to school in the Indianapolis area. It's a lovely city, but it's not known for its tropical beaches!) You would have to scramble to get a hotel room and make additional flight reservations, which would finally get you to Cancun. You would have spent a lot more money than you planned, and it would have taken a lot more time to get there. In the meantime, you would have been frustrated, annoyed, aggravated, angry, and disappointed that your dream vacation had turned into a never-ending nightmare.

Perhaps you're doing the same in your work and life without focusing on what you truly want. You need a vision statement. A vision statement is a description of what you want to create, including your personal and professional aspirations. This is critical, as you can't hit a target if you don't know what it is. Your vision statement is highly personal and must be written in your own words.

Vision statements come in two varieties. Before you write your vision statement, decide which type you prefer. Both will get you where you want to go. It's your decision which version you choose.

Type 1: Realistic Style: This type of vision statement is written based on what you have achieved in the past. One example is that you've made $90,000 this past year and now are shooting for $95,000. Or if you've been to Disneyland on vacation the last two years, you might write that you're traveling to Disneyland again. You've done it before and know you can do it again. Less fear is involved with this type of statement. On the flip side, there's also less excitement, as in some ways you're still staying in your Comfort Zone, meaning you know what to expect on your vacation. You've been there and done it before. A caveat with the realistic style is that because you've done this before, it doesn't require a lot of motivation from you to do it again. As a result, your brain gets bored and lazy, making it hard to exceed that goal.

Type 2: Imaginative Style: I also call this the "Bewitched style." You allow yourself to daydream and get in touch with what would light you up. What dream would make you so excited to know that you are creating it? Maybe you're still going on a Disney vacation, and this time, you're taking one of their cruises or going to Disneyland in France. Doesn't that sound fun to think about that trip happening? Or you decide to go from $90,000 to $125,000 in annual income. Your life would be more impacted by that kind of increase!

A lot of people are afraid to dream big, and there are lots of reasons, which I will cover in upcoming chapters. Some reasons you may be aware of, while others will surprise you.

Again, it's your choice which style of vision statement you choose. However, I highly recommend, especially since you're reading this book, that you decide to go for it and select the imaginative style.

LET'S GET CLARITY

For the following exercise, you'll need to be in a quiet, undisturbed place where you can give yourself some time to slow down and think about what you want to create in your life. When you're ready, get out your journal, and make sure you include the answers to the following questions while writing your vision statement. These answers will help you get the clarity you need to successfully reach your goals.

While you're writing, don't judge, and don't worry about the "how's," as those answers will come later.

Vision statements can be written for any length of time. Some people prefer to focus on 5 to 10 years from now; others prefer a shorter length. I recommend you focus on 12 to 24 months from now. That way, there is some distance, yet it isn't so far out that you can't see your dream on the horizon.

Answer the following questions to create your vision statement:

1. *Work:*
   a. What are the changes in your business/work life?
   b. What is your work style? (Working one-on-one, in a group, remotely, from home, in an office, in a leadership position, as a consultant, as a team player?)
   c. What hours do you want to work? (Monday to Friday with weekends off? Summers off?)
   d. What services/products do you want to offer to earn your income?
   e. What kind of clients/partners/boss do you want?
   f. What type of team/employees/co-workers do you want?

2. *Income:*
   a. What do you want your income to be?

3. *Personal:*
   a. What will you do with this additional income? (Spend, travel, save, donate?)
   b. If you're buying things, what do you want to buy? (For example, car, television, home, renovations?)
   c. If you're traveling, where do you want to go? Do you want a travel companion?
   d. If you're putting the money in the bank, what type of accounts? (Pay off debt, retirement, investments, savings?)
   e. What do you want to do during your free time? (Classes, education, spa, physical activities, family activities?)
   f. Describe your health? Your physical appearance?
   g. What are you doing for fun?

4. *Relationships:*
   a. What changes would happen as a result of this new level in your life?
   b. How would romantic partnerships change?
   c. What types of friendships would you have?

5. *Family:*
   a. What would this new level of success mean to your family?
   b. Is there anything additional you could now provide for your family members?

6. *Community:*
   a. What would this new level of success mean to your community?
   b. Is there anything additional you could now offer your community?

7. *Legacy:*
   a. What would this mean for your legacy?
   b. Would you have any new accolades, honors, awards, degrees, or certifications?

After you've answered all these questions, put them together as if you're writing a letter to someone, telling them what is going on in your life 12 to 24 months from now.

TIME TO REFINE

Now, to refine your vision statement, make sure it includes these points so it will set you up to succeed:

1. *Reread your vision statement.* Does it make you happy to think about this happening in your life? (Hint: You want to have a big smile on your face.)
2. *Add "at least" for amounts mentioned.* For example, I am making at least $100,000 per year. After all, if The Universe wants to bring you more, don't limit yourself.
3. *Make all sentences present tense.* The joy is always on the journey. You want to start feeling how good this is now. You don't want to wait to start feeling good.
4. *Eliminate any "shoulds."* Often, people think they "should" do something because they were told to or because others are doing it. If you don't want it, eliminate it from your statement. Here's the deal: This is your life. You decide how it goes.
5. *Add a sentence using six adjectives sharing how you will feel.* For example, "I'm feeling excited, happy, proud, elated, energized, and successful with the direction of my life."
6. *Reread your statement again.* Does it make you happy, excited, and full of joy to think about this coming to fruition in your life? (Hint: You want to love what you've written.)
7. *Add a closing sentence to your vision statement.* "As it is written, so it shall be," or "This or something better," or a similar statement.

Take your newly created vision statement and write it on a note card or another piece of paper. Place it where you will see it many times a day, as a reminder of the changes that will be happening in your life.

VISION BOARDS

My clients create vision boards to go along with their statements. To create your vision board, you will need poster board, glue, photos, images, and graphics of words to visualize what your future will look like. By doing so, it ignites another part of the brain and helps keep the excitement up for you while you are on your journey. I suggest my clients have mini vision board parties with their partners and children so others start to learn about this process, too. It's a lot of fun!

Can you put the most important part of your vision statement into one sentence, which gives an overview of what you want to create over the next 12 to 24 months?

Write that sentence down and post it in places that you will frequently see it, such as your wallet, dashboard, vision board, and bathroom mirror.

THE BIG QUESTION

Ask yourself: How badly do you want what you've written? Rate it on a scale of zero to 10, zero meaning it doesn't matter and 10 meaning that it is the most important thing. Write that number down. This is the second stage of the Money Zone.

You must have a burning desire that this will happen. Meaning that when it's a cold and rainy day, you're willing to get out of bed and do what needs to be done. When you're tired, you're willing to drive across town to meet someone. Do you want your vision that you just wrote so badly that you will do whatever it takes to make it happen? When you find something you love that much, you don't let anything stand in your way. If not, it won't happen. More about that in the next chapter.

Why must your vision happen? Get clear on your big why and why this is so important for you. This clarity will make your journey so much more comfortable.

BELIEVE IN YOU

Lastly, for the third stage, you must believe that this can and will come true. I was invited to be the keynote/sole guest presenter at a big event in California with over 400 attendees; most had never heard of me before. For an introvert like me, just being invited was an accomplishment. From the start, I held this belief that I would get a standing ovation when I finished. (I hadn't had a standing ovation in this type/ size of venue before.) I did my Laws of Attraction exercises, as well as other mindset techniques (which I will share with you in chapters to come) with my coach to keep my belief up. Guess what? I got my standing ovation. And the applause was thunderous.

Do you believe that your vision statement can and will come true for you? Rate it on a scale of zero to 10. Zero is that you don't believe anything so wonderful would ever happen and 10 that it's almost walking through the door for you. Write that number down. Most people will not write down a 10. And if you did write a "10" it's often because you didn't dream big enough. More about why you do or don't believe this will come true in the next chapter.

KNOCK THOSE BLOCKS DOWN!

Before moving on, take some quiet time to list all the things you believe are in the way or could be in the way of having the success you desire. These could be your fears, doubts, beliefs, worries, or old stories that are real or perceived. I'll be sharing more about your stories later in the book. For now, think of these as what you believe you are (or aren't) capable of, what you deserve, and what type of results you expect to get.

Examples you might list below include: "I don't know how to do it," "I don't have the resources," "It will be too difficult," "I'm not good at that," or "I've failed before."

What's in My Way:

1. _____

2. _____

3. _____

4. _____

5. _____

6. _____

7. _____

8. _____

9. _____

10. _____

Now, go back and rate each one from zero to 10. Zero means it doesn't bother you at all, and if so, cross it off the list. Ten means it keeps you up every night. By listing your obstacles, you're proactively watching out for pitfalls. Throughout the rest of the book, I will be teaching various methods of shifting these blocks, making them less of an obstacle.

In the next chapter, let's move into uncovering blocks that have held you back in the past.

Lessons in Brilliance

✦ The Money Zone is the second step where you develop the clarity, desire, and belief on what you want to create.

✦ Write your vision statement and post it in places where it will frequently be seen. This is your life that you are deliberately creating. If there are parts that don't make you over-the-moon excited, it's time for a rewrite.

✦ Clarity allows you to have a direct path to where you are going.

✦ You must have a burning desire to make your vision statement a reality. That feeling will propel you into action on the days when you are not in the mood. If you don't have this, are you really creating what you want?

✦ A belief in yourself that you can have this is what most people are missing.

✦ Fill out the list of what's in your way. Feel free to go back to this chart and add items as they pop up.

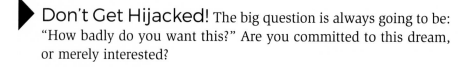 **Don't Get Hijacked!** The big question is always going to be: "How badly do you want this?" Are you committed to this dream, or merely interested?

3

It's Time to Rewrite Your Old Story

This is the perfect time to introduce the concept of "mindset." Some of you may already be familiar with that term, while others are hearing it for the first time. You'll learn in this chapter how mindset is at least 90 percent responsible for your success (or failure).

DUELING MINDS

How many times have you set New Year's resolutions and failed? You had decided that this was going to be the year that you lost weight, went to the gym, made more money, saved more money, found love, spent more time with family, decluttered, etc. How often did you end up giving up on these resolutions within a few weeks or months? You're not alone.

Here's why that happens. Your mind consists of two parts: conscious and subconscious. When you're fully present, you're using your conscious mind; it's what you use to create New Year's resolutions. Your conscious mind loves to be creative and dreams big. It knows you are capable of anything and everything. You declare to the world that this year you will (fill in the blank). It feels good to say those words. It even feels powerful as you start to imagine how fabulous your life will be once you achieve those results. You envision how amazing it all will be.

Then the subconscious mind takes over, and according to neuroscience research, it's a million times more powerful than the conscious mind. All your fears, doubts, beliefs, and old stories are held there. Your subconscious mind's voice starts telling you all the reasons why you shouldn't do this and why you will fail.

Do you remember hearing that little inner voice of yours telling you:

» it's going to be too difficult?
» it's going to be too expensive?
» it's going to take too long?
» you've tried before, and it hasn't worked, so why bother?
» no one in your family has done this?
» none of your friends have done this?
» people may not like you if you do this?

It sounds like your subconscious mind is your worst critic. When in reality, all it wants to do is keep you safe and do things in the easiest way possible. "Easy" is important because the mind likes to conserve energy. It likes to do things it is familiar with and knows how to do. Think of this as similar to "autopilot" on an airplane.

After all, if you've tried to charge more money in the past and it hasn't worked, that would have left you feeling disappointed. Your subconscious mind doesn't want you to feel discouraged again. It's protecting you. So, it's going to save you the trouble by reminding you of all the things that could go wrong and have gone wrong, making you believe that it's better not to proceed forward because it doesn't want you to risk failure again.

THE SUBCONSCIOUS MIND'S ROLE

The subconscious mind is also where you hold your patterns and repetitive behavior. Simply explained, the subconscious mind takes things you learned in your conscious mind and stores them for future reference, which can be good and bad.

The good part is your conscious mind helps you learn how to take action, such as drive a car, write, read, and cook, and then stores it in the subconscious mind so you can perform the task repeatedly. That's how you're able to get in your car and go; you no longer have to think about how to start the engine or where to place your hands.

The subconscious mind even allows you to multitask so you can cook dinner and talk to the people in the room at the same time. Without that part of your brain, can you imagine if you had to say to someone, "Please don't talk to me; I'm drinking water and need to concentrate"?

On the flip side, some studies say that 70 percent of your behavior today is the same as yesterday's and will be the same as tomorrow's. (Are you getting a lightbulb moment of why you're not getting different results?)

When you're in your subconscious mind, it's like running on autopilot. That's how the pilot can leave the cockpit to use the restroom. Technically, the pilot could sleep during most of the flight. In many ways, you're sleeping through your life. Have you ever driven somewhere, and partly through the ride, looked around and wondered how you got there? Guess who's driving? It's your subconscious mind!

The subconscious mind doesn't like to do things differently. It knows the way you've done things in the past and wants to keep doing it that way. It believes the way you've done it before works for you. However, since you're reading this book, you know that the way you've done it before doesn't always work, right?

HOW OUR MIND DEVELOPS

Our mind isn't fully developed for the first six years of our life. At that time, our mind is basically a sponge that absorbs all the information around it from everyone and everything. This means parents, siblings, relatives, television, internet, teachers, books, religion, and so on. The brain isn't able to discern what is good or bad information. It's just information, and that data starts to form how you see the world. If you have relatives who lived through the Great Depression, it is quite possible you are carrying on views of the world based on their experiences. Think about how all these different views have influenced how you show up in the world, what you believe you can achieve, and how you view success.

An example I often share when public speaking is that of a smartphone. Let's say both you and I buy a new phone on the same day at the same store. It's even the same model. You load your music, and I load my music on our individual phones. I have eclectic taste, from jazz and musicals to classical and rock, while your music library is made up entirely of rap.

When I load my music, my phone isn't going to rate each song with a thumbs up or thumbs down. It's not going to tell me that some of my songs are old and not cool. It's just going to load the songs on the phone. It's not even going to ask me why I don't have rap in my library. It takes all the music in and is ready to play it over and over. Your phone will do the same: It will put all your rap in its music library and will never question or comment on your song choices.

Our young brains do the same thing. Whatever we hear, learn, and observe, we take in as the truth. At that young age, we don't have the wherewithal to question, argue, or dispute information. If we hear that "rich people are evil," we accept it and don't bring up all the rich people who are kind, generous, and philanthropists. If we hear that women aren't good at math and science, we don't mention Madame Curie. No, we take it all in and believe it to be the truth. Even when it's not.

Let's take it a step further. You overhear your mom tell your dad that "no one in your family has ever been successful." Unfortunately, you will believe that is your fate, too. When you try to take action that goes above and beyond your Comfort Zone, there will always be that voice pulling you back to keep you aligned with your family's beliefs. Not until you get the support (whether it's from this book, private mentoring, or another resource) to release those beliefs will you be able to move to the next level.

Up to age 6, you're downloading information, just like that smartphone. Some researchers compare those early years to being in a hypnotic state. Those formative years determine how you see the world, how you believe you fit in, and what you deserve.

TWO TYPES OF BELIEFS
I focus on two types of beliefs when working with my clients: limiting beliefs and core beliefs.

Limiting Your Thinking
Limiting beliefs are how you see yourself in relation to the outside world. This is often when people rationalize why they can't do

something or have something. They might tell themselves that task is impossible for them to do. People believe this to be as true as if it's being reported on the evening news.

Limiting beliefs are quite common. The following are some examples; how many times a day do you say any of these phrases?

- » No one in my community would...
- » No one in my industry would...
- » Not in this economy...
- » This time of year, no one would...
- » Most people won't/don't...
- » My company wouldn't like that...
- » That's not how things are done...
- » No one's ever done that before...
- » Women aren't good at this...
- » Men aren't good at this...
- » There's too much competition...
- » There isn't any...
- » There's only enough for some...
- » And so on.

The problem is that when you have these limiting beliefs, they keep you stuck from trying to move forward. One of my clients, Jane, wanted to increase her income. She had been in business for several years, and her family size was increasing. There was no time to delay. I got her focused on a specific niche. We created new product offerings for her clients at double and triple what she had previously been charging. That would easily allow her income to increase to that needed level. At first, she was excited about all this, but then her face and voice started showing doubt. She looked at me and said, "No one in my industry would EVER charge this much." That was her limiting belief holding her back. If we hadn't been able to work on that together and release it, she wouldn't have been able to move forward and increase her income.

Getting to Your Core

There's a second part of this story: Jane's core beliefs surfaced and started messing with her newfound confidence. Core beliefs are how you view and compare yourself to others. It's what you believe about yourself. Here are common examples of core beliefs:

» I'm not smart enough.
» I'm not good enough.
» I'm not pretty enough.
» People will get mad at me.
» People won't like me.
» I've never done this before.
» It's never worked for me before.
» I'm not good at this.
» I'm not good at handling money.
» I always screw up.
» And so on.

Jane was worried that her clients would get mad and not hire her if she charged more money. We all have a basic need to be liked and loved. This comes from our childhood, where every little girl and boy wants to be loved by their parents. Any time we feel that something might threaten that love, it may stop us from taking action.

So, Jane and I did more mindset work to release that fear. I also helped ease her comfort level by teaching her what to say to her clients. As a result, she was able to triple her income that year, easily support her new family member, and improve her lifestyle. If she hadn't done this mindset work, she would have let her fears and doubts keep her stuck in an unsatisfactory financial lifestyle.

Fears, doubts, beliefs, and old stories are why so many people stay stuck. Maybe that's been you in the past. The good news is that it's time to return that old story to the library and write a new one.

DON'T TOUCH THAT DIAL

In the previous chapter, I talked about creating imagination-style vision statements. One of the reasons so many are uncomfortable with dreaming big is because they have placed limits on their life. At an early age, this starts with the word "no." Most people have heard that word over 60,000 times before age 3. Think about how many times that means you've heard no over your entire life!

As a child, you most likely heard:

» No!
» Don't touch that!
» Don't do that!
» Wait!
» Wait until you're older!
» Wait until you're bigger!
» You're going to hurt yourself!
» Be careful!
» Stop!
» Stop. Let someone help you!
» No! No! No!

If you went ahead and took that action, despite the warnings, most likely you were punished or told you were bad. Think about the child who picks up a glass figurine, is told no by an adult, but still proceeds. Unfortunately, the child drops the figurine, and it shatters into hundreds of pieces.

Years ago, the child would have been spanked or punished and told they were bad. This facilitates the belief that the child is bad, not that their action is bad. Over and over, throughout their life, the child will hear the words in their subconscious mind that they are bad. You can see how low self-confidence can be perpetuated in this young child, allowing them to believe that they are bad and unworthy of future success and happiness. All because they dropped a piece of glass.

Hearing no so many times in your life has created barriers of what you are willing to do and what you think you can have. These words play over and over in your subconscious mind.

Now, instead of an adult telling you those words, you're saying no to yourself. It excited your conscious mind to think about the possibility of doubling or tripling your income. On the flip side, your subconscious mind is saying, "Who do you think you are? You're not worth that much money," and as a result of that internal message, you've said no to trying to move forward, and kept yourself stuck. All this happens in a nanosecond in your mind.

START WITH AWARENESS

The first step to making a change is awareness. The reason is that once you become aware, then you can choose whether you want to do something about these fears, doubts, beliefs, and old stories or leave things status quo. It's always your choice. Go or Don't Go.

Take a few minutes in a nice, quiet place, and start listing your limiting and core beliefs. Don't judge yourself. Just write.

My limiting beliefs about the world are:

1. _____

2. _____

3. _____

4. _____

5. _____

6. _____

7. _____

8. _____

9. _____

10. _____

My core beliefs about myself are:

1. _____

2. _____

3. _____

4. _____

5. _____

6. _____

7. _____

8. _____

9. _____

10. _____

Now, go back and rate how strongly each one bothers you. You will again use a scale of zero to 10, with zero meaning it doesn't bother you at all (cross it off your list) and 10 that it keeps you awake at night.

These are your blocks, worries, and stuck points. Unless you want to be permanently stuck in these areas, you must release these thoughts and replace them with a more positive belief about the world, how you fit in, and how you view yourself.

You might kid yourself by going through what I call the "good month/bad month" syndrome. That's where things start to look up, and then you go backward. One step forward and two steps back. It's because you feel safer in your Comfort Zone, and your fears, doubts, and worries are popping up and pushing you back. More about that in the upcoming chapters.

TAPPING TO YOUR SUCCESS

One of my favorite ways to shift these blocks is through the powerful mindset technique of tapping, which I am an expert in. To use this method, you are guided to tap on specific meridian points on your upper body and face while reciting certain phrases I give you to say. This process allows your negative thoughts to shift into positive ones.

Visit www.KateBeeders.com/LearnToTap and experience tapping first-hand with my tapping video, script, and audio.

I first learned about tapping while on a trip to the Caribbean. You know how it is on vacation. You'll try new things, taste new types of foods, and experience new kinds of adventures. On my way out from a meditation class, I complimented the instructor. He had this lovely melodic voice that made it easy for me to enjoy the meditation.

Offhandedly, I lamented to him that if only he could teach me a way to quit eating ice cream, my day would be perfect. He looked at me, puzzled, and asked what I meant. I explained that I live in Boston, where we have ice cream shops on every street corner that are open year-round. This makes ice cream an irresistible temptation for me.

Ever since working in an ice cream shop as a part-time job in high school with my best friend, ice cream has been my weakness. I would love to eat ice cream every day of the week, but that is not healthy.

His eyes lit up, and he asked if I wanted to try a new technique. I figured why not, as I had nothing to lose. He proceeded to try something with me that quite honestly I had no clue how it worked, and I didn't even remember the name. But in the brief time I tried it, I had a significant shift, in which my desire for ice cream had faded. I had just as much interest in eating ice cream as I did in eating a metal stapler. I thanked him and went on my way to enjoy the beautiful Caribbean beach.

Back at home, a few weeks later, I experienced a very upsetting situation at work. My boss called me on the phone and told me that he could no longer do all the things he promised to do for me when I accepted a position at his company. He explained the company was merging and would be going in a different direction. All those things he promised me were deal-breakers, which was the reason I had left my previous company earlier that year. I was so angry at him for breaking his word to me.

He asked me to meet him in the office the next morning to further discuss the situation. I was fuming and didn't know what to do. A little voice inside of me suggested reaching out to my contact in the Caribbean and asking if his technique could help me. Over Skype, without even knowing how the method worked or its name, he helped me release all my anger and frustration in a short time.

In those days, Skype didn't work very well, as you could hear an echo and it was always cutting off. Yet I still got excellent results with tapping. I met with my boss the next morning. I was calm, and he was calm. He ended up offering me more money and a few other additional benefits to make up for the situation, which I accepted. We both left the meeting feeling as if we had won.

If I hadn't experienced tapping, I can promise you that I would have gone into the meeting angry, and my boss would have been upset. The result would not have been a pretty picture, and neither of us would have won.

Over the next few months, I connected with my contact in the Caribbean for more tapping, until I made the decision that I wanted to be an expert in this technique. As someone who is very results-oriented and tends to be more strategic, I was surprised about how passionate I became about this energy technique, and I wanted to know all about it. That led me to spend tens of thousands of dollars learning all I could. What's so interesting about this method is that it has helped millions of people worldwide get unstuck, whether it's something relatively simple, like the food craving I started with, or something as complex as PTSD (post-traumatic stress disorder).

As a Boston native, I would never have guessed that I would build a business around a mindset technique in a city that is quite provincial and action-oriented. Yet here I am.

The following are some of the many areas that I've helped my clients with through the use of tapping:

- » public speaking
- » charging what you're worth
- » going on "unplugged" vacations
- » setting and keeping boundaries
- » expanding current businesses
- » increasing your confidence
- » implementing new systems
- » clarity in your vision
- » delegating
- » procrastination
- » understanding your big "why"
- » firing clients
- » better self-care
- » hiring and firing team members
- » sales conversations
- » showing up as a leader
- » networking
- » asking for raises
- » asking for what is needed

- » learning when to say yes and no
- » trying new things
- » attracting ideal clients
- » having a right to be seen and heard
- » stress and overwhelm
- » being seen in the public eye
- » focus
- » creating better partnerships
- » and many other fears, doubts, beliefs and old stories

With tapping, I can help clients quickly shift out of uncomfortable situations and negative patterns. I make it look easy, yet there's a lot going on behind the scenes.

A lot of people using tapping have learned it from less-than-reputable sources or online. I urge you to make sure that when you try tapping, you work with an expert (like me), who has trained personally under the top people in this field. Dealing with someone's mindset is a serious matter and shouldn't be learned over the internet. Otherwise, you can do a lot of harm to someone.

Go ahead and try tapping (www.KateBeeders.com/LearnToTap) and watch the intensity of your blocks decrease.

In the next chapter, you'll learn how to start seeing yourself actually achieving these results.

Lessons in Brilliance

- ✦ The conscious mind is when you are creative and present.
- ✦ The subconscious mind holds your fears, doubts, beliefs, and old stories. It's a million times more powerful than the conscious mind. Often, people will fail at their goals due to their strong fears, doubts, beliefs, and old stories that pop up.
- ✦ Limiting beliefs are how you see yourself in relationship to the rest of the world.
- ✦ Core beliefs are what you believe about yourself and what you are capable of achieving.
- ✦ Awareness is the first step. Then it's up to you to choose to change. You'll get different results when you take those next steps to release and replace the negative thoughts holding you back.
- ✦ In my experience, tapping is the most powerful and fastest way to shift someone's mindset. Experience tapping and see what transforms for you: www.KateBeeders.com/LearnToTap

▶ **Don't Get Hijacked!** You can't see the tip of your own nose. Sometimes, what you think is keeping you stuck is only the tip of the iceberg. Often, when you look at your life through your own lenses, it is challenging to see precisely where you are stuck. It takes an expert to find it for you and guide you through the release.

4

Make Your Decisions from Your Destination

Let's talk about money. That's what everyone thinks they want more of, right? Don't you believe that if you had more money, all your problems would be solved? One of my clients, Sara, used to believe that, and boy, is it not true. That's because she didn't understand money. Sara thought it was all about being able to buy whatever she wanted when she wanted it. She couldn't figure out why she had a love/hate relationship with money.

Here's how to define money: It's a currency used to trade for services or products. Before money originated, one person would trade something of theirs for something of someone else's. Perhaps trading cows for sheep? Now, we trade our money for internet services or a new computer or food or books. People trade their money for my coaching services, and I trade my money to pay my mortgage. All we are doing is exchanging energy—trading one thing for another.

WHO'S GOT THE POWER?

Many years ago, it was decided that whoever had the most money had the most power. And so it began. Ever since then, people have been trying to keep up with their neighbors, co-workers, and whomever they see online or on social media. Lack of money often causes them to think less of themselves:

» in comparison to someone who has more money (or objects).
» when they have less money in the bank.
» if they don't drive a car as nice as their neighbor's or co-worker's.
» if their home isn't as big or expensive as their neighbor's or co-worker's.

Years ago, when I was lamenting that I wish I had more, an accountant I worked with at the time told me, "Don't wish for what your neighbors have. Often, it's an illusion. I see how much money they really have and it's typically not as much as you think."

Isn't that crazy? We give all our power away because of pieces of paper with numbers written on them.

If all of us went to the bank and asked for our money in cash right now, the bank wouldn't have it on hand. There's more in circulation and being spent than exists!

I've got news for you. If you let money rule your life, you're operating from a middle-class mindset, which will never make you wealthy. A middle-class mindset around money is often inherited from previous generations who lived through the Great Depression and other catastrophic times. Due to what they experienced, their fears around money grew exponentially, and those beliefs were passed on to future generations. Beliefs such as "saving for a rainy day" and others cause you to have a fear-based mindset around money.

Depending on your money mindset, your self-confidence can go up and down based on your bank account. Up one day and down the next. Who wants to live that way? I certainly don't!

To become prosperous, you need to change that mindset. Let's talk about how.

WHAT'S YOUR MONEY STORY?

Your money story is how you view money and your relationship to it. Often, most people's stories are based around fear and doubt, as they don't really understand money. To uncover your beliefs around money, you need a clear understanding of what your relationship is with it and what you desire. Throughout this chapter, I'll ask you to answer questions on this topic.

Money is merely an outcome. It's a result of a combination of things. Being the smartest or hardest-working person isn't enough to make you wealthy. Often those characteristics can hold you back. One of the biggest laments I often hear from entrepreneurs is that others are making more money than they are, yet they believe those people have less talent than them. What they don't realize is there is a reason for that success.

Take a few minutes in a quiet place to answer the following questions:

1. What is your income this year?
2. What would you like your income to be in 12 to 24 months?
3. Have you ever made that much money?

For you to make more money than you have in the past, you will need to change how you do things and how you show up in your brilliance. As the expression goes, "If you want different results, you must do things differently." More about how this works in future chapters, but for now, here is a definition of what I mean by the term "show up in your brilliance": The dictionary describes "brilliance" as "an intense brightness of light or exceptional talent or intelligence." That's not the definition I am referring to. It's not about wearing a certain outfit, makeup, or hairstyle. It's also not about how smart you are. It's more about an inner glow and an inner knowing or confidence you have. It is when you're doing things that make sense to you and are aligned with who you are and your gifts. It is when you are able to attract people to you without trying and when you're going with the flow instead of against it. You give yourself permission to dream big. It is also when you fully understand that you have a right to be seen and heard. As a result, you have amazing opportunities, abundance, and happiness in your life, and you become a beacon of light for others.

Your beliefs around money are one of the biggest factors regarding your income level. Are you curious what your money story is? It isn't about your income, how much money you have in the bank, or how much debt you have. Understanding how your money story affects most of your decisions throughout the day is empowering.

To find your money story, start by answering this question.

Money is...

1. _____

2. _____

3. _____

4. _____

5. _____

6. _____

7. _____

8. _____

9. _____

10. _____

You might have answered that money is unreliable, hard to get, difficult to hold on to, only for some people, or similar answers.

Next, answer the following questions honestly. Write your thoughts in your journal. Remember not to judge your answers. There is no right or wrong. You're looking for your starting point to change from here. Put the answers to all your questions together as you start to write your money story.

1. How do you make decisions to spend money? What do you buy/not buy?
2. How do you view money?
3. How often do you worry about money?
4. How does money make you feel?

5. What do you believe about wealthy people?
6. What did your family teach you about money?
7. How did your parents spend money?
8. Do you pay cash, use credit cards, borrow money?
9. Do you have a budget?
10. Do you have a savings account?
11. Do you pay your bills early? On time? Late?
12. How does your religion view money and wealth?

Reread your money story after you've written it in your journal. How does it make you feel? Are you starting to see patterns in these areas?

» How you spend money
» How you save money
» How you earn money
» How you feel when you see your bank account balance

As you get more clarity in these areas, you'll start to notice when and where you're giving your power away to money.

Jenny, a rising star in her company, had been offered an important promotion and impressive raise to go along with it. Instead of being excited about her success, she wasn't able to sleep at night due to her worries. She told me that money had always been tight when she was growing up, and it was a source of stress for her parents. In fact, money was the only subject that caused arguments. Other than that, her parents appeared to be happily married.

When she was a teenager, her father received a promotion that involved a lot more responsibility at work. He would often miss family dinners and celebrations. The tension between her parents grew and grew until, ultimately, they decided to divorce.

Jenny thought of herself as happily married and was terrified of what this financial increase would do to her relationship with her husband. She feared reliving what her parents experienced at the end of their marriage. Her belief was that money causes relationships to fall apart and end.

Not until I helped her examine her relationship with money was Jenny able to create a new story of how she could earn more money, and it didn't have to harm her marriage.

A huge key to having more abundance (success, money, opportunities, love, etc.) in your life is to take personal responsibility and understand that what you have is what you created, whether it was deliberate or not. Learn to use money as a tool and resource instead of letting it be in charge of you. Once that happens, you become a weak, powerless victim. You can't be successful and be a victim at the same time. It's one or the other. You choose.

If you would like additional information on your money story, take my online quiz: www.KateBeeders.com/MoneyStoryQuiz

CHANGING YOUR STORY

You're here because you want a new money story. I'm going to teach you how to write a great one and how to live it, too.

Take some quiet, undisturbed time and write your new money story. Make sure to include what changes you now have in your life and what positive emotions (happy, freedom, proud, calm, etc.) you would have. Start to feel what you are creating as if it is happening now.

Recently, when I taught this topic at my Money Acceleration Retreat™, my attendees decided that they wanted to be in partnership with money. By partnership, they meant that they understood how money works, and they treat it respectfully instead of fearfully. What do you want?

My new money story is:

_____

_____

_____

_____

_____

_____

THE LAWS OF ATTRACTION

It's crucial for you to know about the Laws of Attraction and how they can help you attract more abundance into your life. Essentially, the Laws of Attraction say that what you focus on, think about, or believe is what you will attract into your life. Although there are many laws, I want to focus on only four for this book.

Law of Manifestation

You attract what you focus your attention on. Years ago, when I worked in downtown Boston, I had a boss who drove a fancy black Porsche convertible. Whenever he would drive us to prospective client meetings, he would always ask, "Where's my parking spot?" Sure enough, no matter what time of day it was, he always found a parking space in front of the building we were going to. It never failed. Do you know the odds of that happening? To find an ideal parking spot in the downtown area of a busy city during the weekday? It's near impossible. Not for my boss. He believed he would find a space, and sure enough, he always did.

When I taught this law to my client, Ann, she began to manifest all sorts of things in her life. First, she tried it over the holiday season at her mall parking lot. It is nearly unthinkable to find a spot in a decent location at this mall any time of year—never mind over the holiday season. Imagine her surprise when she saw a space in front of the mall entrance. Not just once, but on several of her shopping excursions.

That wasn't the end of things for Ann—it was merely the beginning of her understanding what is possible. Inside the mall, she started noticing that the items on her gift list were on sale. They were things that she had already planned on buying before she had entered the store.

She wanted to escape the cold, gray winter and had her heart set on a sunny Caribbean vacation at an upscale resort. However, she didn't have the money put aside for the trip. Ann set the intention to create this vacation on a Friday. She started to put together a plan for how she could come up with the money. Lo and behold, in the mail on Saturday was an envelope from this resort, offering her three free nights and airfare. Honestly, I couldn't make this stuff up.

Now, Ann wanted to amp things up and try for something bigger. She had an ideal car in mind, but it was expensive and not one she would typically buy. Ann went through the steps I taught her: deciding which car she wanted and what features, and putting it on her vision board. She imagined what it would be like to drive the car and what her view would be like from the driver's seat. She also determined how much she was willing to pay for the car. She started noticing the car she wanted on the road; wherever she looked, it popped up in the exact color and model. Then she was ready for the final step. Ann went to a dealership where they had the precise make and model she desired. She bought it that day, because it was for the exact amount she had predetermined, whereas elsewhere it was selling for $10,000 more.

In the years since, Ann has used this same process to manifest more vacations, new jobs, renovations for her home, and even a closer relationship with her husband and other family members. Before we met, Ann didn't think any of this was possible. This works!

Law of Magnetism

You can only attract the same type of energy you are putting out. One comment I hear repeatedly from attendees of my events and retreats is that I attract the best community. I must admit that is true.

People make best friends that they keep for years. No one wants to leave and sever the connections. It's not luck. (I don't believe in luck.) I truly believe it's because I set an intention of who I want to attend. I also set an intention of what I am providing at the event and create a safe space for this to happen. I know that exactly the right people will be in the room, ready to learn. It must be!

Another way the Law of Magnetism will show up is in experiences. Let's say a friend invites you to join him for dinner at a particular restaurant. You reply that every time you go to that restaurant, the parking is terrible, you wait in line, the food is cold, and the server is slow. Well, your friend persuades you to meet him anyway. Sure enough, the parking is terrible, you wait in line, the food is cold, and the server is slow. What you expect is what you will attract.

Law of Pure Desire

Your intentions must be pure, not manipulative. We've all heard stories about used-car salesmen. I hate to throw them under the bus, but the reason they have a bad reputation is the belief that they are trying to make money by telling you untruths about the condition of the cars they are trying to sell.

Years ago, this happened to me when I went to what I thought was a reputable dealership to buy a "gently used" car. The salesperson didn't tell me that the car had previously been in an accident. I had 17 problems in 11 days, including the car dying on a major four-lane highway in Boston during rush hour traffic—talk about a near-death experience!

The dealership ended up giving me a new car. The sales manager, who was so upset with how the process had gone, ultimately left the industry, as he didn't like the lack of the code of ethics he was asked to operate under. I'm not saying every car salesperson is like that; this is an example. Unfortunately, the bad ones stick out like thorns.

In this situation, the used-car salesman had been more interested in making a sale instead of being truthful and telling me the car had been in an accident. If he had been following this law, he would have wanted me to find a car that would make me happy and keep me safe.

Another example of this law is in the dating world. Let's say you give a prospective romantic partner a gift in hopes of getting something in return. You're not giving out of pure desire to make that person happy. You're giving to get something. It doesn't work. It always comes back to bite you.

Law of Paradoxical Intent

In this law, you get the very thing you didn't want to happen. Do you remember fearing in high school that the person you liked wouldn't call? This situation is an excellent example of how the Law of Paradoxical Intent works. You fear that they won't call, and you worry about it. You even have conversations with all your friends to discuss the situation. Will they or won't they call? It takes up every waking minute of your thoughts. Sure enough, they don't call. The reason is because you're putting out so much negative energy around this issue that there is no way it will happen.

This could also happen with a job promotion, prospective client, or new opportunity—anywhere in your life. Your fears, doubts, beliefs, and stories you tell yourself will stop the very thing you want to happen from coming into your life, and instead you'll receive what you were most fearing.

The Laws of Attraction are at work all the time, whether you choose to use them or not. Just like gravity, they exist. When you learn to use them to create a more abundant life, everything changes for you.

YOUR MONEY STORY AND THE LAWS OF ATTRACTION

What is so interesting about your money story is that most of the time you aren't even aware of how it impacts you. Most likely, it affects the majority of your decisions, even in small ways, such as what restaurants you go to and the food you buy. Remember that your money story is also always there, like gravity. It doesn't matter whether you can see it or not. It exists, and it's a program that your mindset is operating under.

One final point to remember is that there is more than enough abundance to go around. Often, people think there is a limited quantity—that some can have it while others can't. That's not true. Everyone can have as much abundance in their life as they desire, without it hurting or taking away from others.

Years ago, Eastern Airlines operated an hourly shuttle between Boston and New York, and between New York and Washington, D.C. Reservations were not required. You merely showed up, and you got a seat. If the plane held 177 people, and you were the 178th, they would pull out a new plane. No questions asked. There weren't limited seats. Everyone got to go. Think of abundance in the same way. There's a seat for everyone.

Most people tend to view abundance the other way and come from a scarcity mindset. When you believe there isn't enough for you, there won't be enough for you. That belief will stop you from moving forward.

Start to make your decisions from your destination, not your starting point.

In the next chapter, you'll learn how to show up in your brilliance and how that changes everything in your life for the better.

Lessons in Brilliance

+ What is your current money story? This is important, as you need to know your starting point. Take this short quiz to get even more insight: www.KateBeeders.com/MoneyStoryQuiz
+ What do you want your new money story to be? This is about your relationship with money. What kind of partnership are you creating?
+ How can you use the Laws of Attraction to bring more abundance into your life?
+ How many times a day do you make decisions about spending money based on what's in your bank account instead of what's best for you?

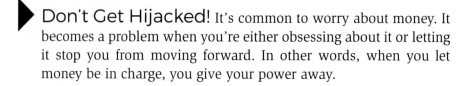 **Don't Get Hijacked!** It's common to worry about money. It becomes a problem when you're either obsessing about it or letting it stop you from moving forward. In other words, when you let money be in charge, you give your power away.

5

Your Four Quadrants of Brilliance™

I bet you wish you could just sit around and hope and pray that all the money, opportunities, and other forms of abundance would just fall from the ceiling and come to you. I wish I could tell you that were possible. But you also have to take initiative, which is why in this chapter we're focusing on the third zone in the Money Acceleration System™: the Action Zone.

As a recovering Type A (aka overachiever), I would typically get excited about the prospect of telling you to take action, especially lots of action. After all, the more action you take, the better off you are, right? Wrong! If you're a Type A, you know that taking action feels good and makes you think you're in control. However, it also creates a tremendous amount of pressure on you to feel the need always to be taking action. Success is more about finding that balance of mindset and effort to bring you those fabulous results you desire.

For most of us, there aren't enough hours in the day to do all that we'd like to accomplish. Between professional, personal, family, and community activities, obligations, and goals, we're kept pretty busy. It's also not about throwing spaghetti against the wall and seeing what sticks. So, when I talk about taking action, it's not necessarily about working harder. It's about working smarter.

I can hear your sigh of relief. If you work harder, rather than smarter, overwhelm and stress will move to the forefront, which means you won't be able to make the best decisions.

Pull out and review your vision statement daily that you wrote at the beginning of this book. Only choose to take action if it aligns with what you wrote and will get you closer to your desires. This clarity and focus helps you deliberately create your life.

FOCUS, FOCUS, FOCUS

One of my clients, Laura, loved the tapping that we did together during her coaching calls, as she benefited from tremendous shifts. She asked my opinion about learning how to do it so she could use it with her clients. It would have been the cherry on the sundae in her business. But as we discussed it, weighed the pros and cons, and talked about her goals, she realized that tapping didn't fit in at the time.

It also became clear that Laura was an avid learner (like many of us), and she wanted to learn more. However, by learning tapping, she would be avoiding foundational business practices, such as networking and sales conversations. When Laura became aware that she was looking for a distraction, she had to laugh. She decided to focus on business practices that would bring in more income for her, rather than learn another skill.

While writing her vision statement, another one of my clients, Tara, had confided that her relationship with her husband was the most important thing in her life. She wanted a weekly date night with him so they could continue to bond and bring romance into their 15-year marriage, since it wasn't in the best shape. In fact, Tara was frightened that they were heading for a divorce.

When a friend invited Tara to go to the movies on her typical date night, she accepted. I asked why she was giving up her date night, as her relationship with her husband was her number-one priority. Tara responded that she didn't want her friend to get mad at her. I helped Tara become aware how this would affect her husband and how she wasn't focused on her number-one priority. She called her friend and switched her plans. That helped Tara start to make more of her own decisions and prioritize what mattered to her. I'm happy to report that several years later, Tara and her husband have never been closer.

What has always worked for me and what I teach my clients is to work from the end backward. In other words, have a picture in your mind of what you want to achieve, and then strategize what action is needed to make it happen.

HOW TO CREATE AN ACTION PLAN THAT WORKS

Whenever my siblings and I got overwhelmed with our school assignments, my mother suggested that we create a list, break things down, and only focus on one task at a time. It worked wonderfully. Now, I'll teach you how to do that.

1. What is your desired result?
2. Set a deadline/due date when the result must happen.
3. Make a list of all the components that are required to pull your plan together. Some people use a flowchart, mind map, or diagram. It doesn't matter which style you use, as long as you're comfortable with the process.
4. Ask for/hire support for the areas you need help.
5. Break down those components more into tiny, manageable tasks and details.
6. Prioritize all the tasks and give them a deadline/due date.
7. Delegate as many tasks as you can. If there isn't something you can delegate regarding this project, is there someone else to whom you can transfer another task to free up your time? One of my clients was writing a book, and most of the tasks required her advanced skills. She asked her children to help more around the house, which gave her more writing time. Get creative. Make this work!
8. Add the tasks to your monthly, daily, and weekly calendars to keep you on track.
9. Set up weekly or biweekly check-ins with your coach/mentor, or ask an accountability buddy to keep you focused.
10. Create small rewards for yourself to keep energized and focused. They can be little things and don't need to cost money.

I teach my clients that the "money is in the follow-up." This means they could make a great connection, give a wonderful speech, or host a fabulous workshop, but if they don't follow up with people afterward and ask for what they want (e.g., sale, promotion, opportunity, introduction), they could be leaving lots of money on the table.

Often, people will hire me because they are disappointed and discouraged that the year didn't work out for them the way they had desired. There's an old expression: "Fail to plan, and you plan to fail." It's imperative you understand the importance of planning and implementing.

QUARTERLY ACTION PLANNING

Every three months, I meet with my clients in my private coaching group to plan out their next quarter. They map out their vision, action steps, and even areas that could be pitfalls. This includes listing what worked and didn't work for them. More about that in upcoming chapters. I recommend you start implementing quarterly planning in your professional and business life.

It's up to you how detailed you want to be. If you want to lose weight, it might be as simple as marking three days on your calendar each week to work out at the gym. Or you can add more, including hiring a nutritionist, reading wellness books, having healthy meals delivered to you, hiring a workout coach, and so on.

If you're an entrepreneur and you want to create a new program, you can start by adding the launch date to your calendar. Then you'll want to add in creating the program, designing a sales page, writing the marketing materials/emails, promoting it in social media ads, choosing the software needed, delegating tasks to your team, and much more.

You must take action to make your dreams come true. To use my airline analogy, a plane can't just sit on the runway and get to its desired destination. It must take off!

DO, DELEGATE, OR DELETE

It's time to introduce the Four Quadrants of Brilliance™ chart, which will help you determine what actions to do, delegate, or delete. The idea behind the chart is to help you understand where you truly shine. Once you know that, you'll want to spend your time focused on those areas. As a result, you'll notice more abundance in your life and your happiness significantly increasing when your actions match your brilliance.

THE FOUR QUADRANTS OF BRILLIANCE™

BRILLIANCE	Like It	Tolerate It	Dislike It

Take some quiet time to fill out the above chart by writing your various activities in each of the columns. The best way to do this is to use this chart for a week, and write down each task that you perform in the appropriate column. Further details about each of the four chart quadrants are provided below.

Dislike It Column

These are the tasks that you truly don't want to do. I remember one of the first website designers I worked with offered to teach me how to use WordPress when it was first becoming popular. I had no interest in it. He thought learning it was a great idea because it would save me money knowing how to make my own changes instead of hiring him for every task I needed done. As a newbie entrepreneur, my focus was on growing my business and making money—not saving money. Learning WordPress went immediately into the "Dislike It" column. I didn't even have to think twice about that one.

One of my clients hated sending out a monthly newsletter. The reason for this is she felt technically challenged. Although she loved to write the articles, she dreaded formatting each one into her newsletter. In fact, for about a week beforehand, she started getting stressed and overwhelmed just thinking about the task. On the actual day, it would take her four hours to do the formatting, and she would be completely frustrated throughout the entire experience. I suggested she hire someone to do this task for her. She was surprised how little it cost her to get this task off her plate and how much she got back in return. She considered hiring this person a great investment! She found the perfect assistant who spent less than an hour on her task, freeing her up to do the things she enjoyed most.

Tolerate It Column

These are the tasks you are willing to do, but you don't enjoy. You do them because they must be done. One of my clients dreaded doing weekly laundry. Imagine how freed up she felt when she included a weekly trip to the laundromat, which washed, folded, and ironed her laundry. She released a lot of undue stress by making this switch.

Like It Column

These tasks are often confused with your "BRILLIANCE" tasks. These are things you enjoy doing, and you do them well. What's missing is the love. I find this often in the coaching world; a lot of people become coaches because they want to help people. Initially, they want as many clients as possible. Then, at a certain point, they realize they don't want to work with a lot of people individually. Maybe it's too draining, takes up too much time, or other reasons. They still want to help people, but in a different form of delivery. Often, that's when they'll create online or big programs so they can continue to be of service in a different way.

BRILLIANCE Column

These are the tasks you would do morning, noon, and night, whether you got paid for them or not (I do want you to get paid for them!). You take for granted how easily these tasks come to you. These are the times when the words that come out of your mouth are so exceptionally brilliant, you hope that someone was around to record them. No one is better than you in these areas. Some people refer to their brilliance as their superpower.

My "BRILLIANCE" column includes the areas of: private coaching; creating powerful strategies; public speaking; leading my retreats; honing in quickly on where/why someone is stuck; releasing fears, doubts, and old stories; facilitating breakthroughs to the next level and beyond; teaching sales enrollment; hosting private events; and creating the best-ever community.

The reason I can be so sure of my areas of brilliance is my clients constantly remind me of my superpowers. Also, I feel and know my brilliance in my heart.

GETTING TO YOUR BRILLIANCE

Once your Four Quadrants of Brilliance™ chart is filled out, the next step is to focus on each column. The goal is to get rid of each item, column by column, until you're living and working solely in your brilliance.

Start with your "Dislike It" column. Prioritize these items, beginning with the one that bothers you the most. How can you remove it from your plate? Hire someone? Delegate it? Stop doing it? Now, do the same in the other columns.

I recommend you pull your Four Quadrants of Brilliance™ chart out at least twice a year and review it, as your attitude toward these items may change as you grow. For example, I moved using Word-Press from my "Dislike It" column into my "Tolerate It" column. Years later, I had my website switched over to WordPress and learned some of the basics. Initially, the reason I had held off is I thought of myself as technically challenged. After all, coming from the corporate world, I didn't do any of this stuff. There was always someone around to handle my technology needs.

About a year after I was first approached to learn WordPress, I happened to be doing some tapping with one of my coaches, and the technology issue came up. I was able to release my belief of being technically challenged and start viewing myself differently. I became more open to trying various types of technology and less worried about failing. Things shifted. Now, when I make technology decisions, it's based on what's best for me, not what I believe about myself. Making that switch put me into a much more powerful position. No more letting that core belief hold me back.

SIMPLIFY YOUR LIFE

Make sure that what's in your "BRILLIANCE" column is what you truly love. After all, the goal is to spend most of your time on these activities. By doing so, you're simplifying your life and allowing the abundance to flow faster and easier.

Remember, as you're working with this chart, just because you know how to do something doesn't mean you should do it. I know how to clean my home; however, I hire someone to do this job, as it's not something I enjoy and it frees me to work in my Zone of Brilliance. Also, every time you hire someone, you're circulating money into the economy, and that's a very good thing.

As you're putting things in your "Dislike It" or "Tolerate It" columns, consider if it's because you don't like it or because you have fears around it. If you don't like it, super. It's important to be aware of this and find a way to not spend your time there. But if it's fear, like the one I had of WordPress, that allows you the choice to get help to release it and come back at it from a place of power. Your choice... Go or Don't Go!

In the chapters to come, you will learn that you should only take action that matches your future self-image. Stay tuned as this will be unveiled to you shortly.

Lessons in Brilliance

✦ In the Action Zone, it's time to decide what actions are the most important ones for you to take to move you closer to your goal.
✦ Strategize action plans to keep you on track, from start to finish.
✦ Use the Four Quadrants of Brilliance™ to uncover where you should be spending your time. For everything else, delegate or delete it.

▶ **Don't Get Hijacked!** Make sure what you are deleting is truly because you dislike it, not because you have a core or limiting belief around it. Sometimes that will be easy for you to know; other times you will need your mentor to guide you.

6

Good Enough Is Good Enough

The fourth step, the Freak-out Zone, is in some ways the most important phase of the Money Acceleration System™. This is where most people fail, quit, or run back to their Comfort Zone.

My Dad was a dentist and taught me all about preventive care and how it was important to brush my teeth after each meal. I inherited his focus on preventive care and how it can make a difference in leading a happy and successful life. You can also practice a little prevention and avoid running back to your Comfort Zone.

IT'S GONE

Have you seen a child on an airplane drop a toy on takeoff, then scream bloody murder until they got it back? Due to the angle of the plane at takeoff, the precious stuffed animal or toy fell out of their hands and rolled toward the back of the aircraft. The child is terrified they'll never see their beloved toy again.

You, as the adult, know that all you need to do is wait for the plane to level off, and you can retrieve the toy. Or perhaps someone will even bring the toy back to you. You know the situation is not that big of a deal. You just have to wait a few minutes and everything will be OK. However, listening to the child cry and scream sounds more like the situation will last a lifetime. That child is in their Freak-out Zone.

The child is distraught about the loss of their toy. You know how to get the toy, but the child doesn't. Once the child gets the toy back, all is good. The crisis has been averted.

Could you imagine for a moment if the plane had to turn around and fly back to the starting point because that child didn't have their toy? Imagine the mayhem that would follow with everyone else on board.

You're not that little child anymore. However, when there's a problem and you don't know the solution, you go into the Freak-out Zone. You might not cry or throw a temper tantrum, but you will certainly change your mood, and as a result, the action you choose to (not) take.

RATIONALIZE OR RATIONAL LIES

Years ago, I worked a short time for a disorganized company. The owner was always yelling and throwing items from his desk when things weren't going his way. He acted like a little child throwing a temper tantrum. He was in the Freak-out Zone. Once he got the solution he needed, he calmed down.

Then there was one of my clients, Jane, who was excited about changing her coaching business model from hourly services to a three-month program. She felt energized that she would finally be able to charge what she was worth. However, the first person she gave her new pricing to told her she was too expensive and declined the offer.

Jane was disappointed and scared, and decided in a nanosecond that it wasn't a good thing to raise her pricing. She "knew" that the person she had been speaking to would have hired her at her old pricing. She was running back to her Comfort Zone, where she felt safe.

Safe feels familiar. The problem is that there isn't any growth in the Comfort Zone. It's all about the illusion of trying to keep things the same. Your brain resists change. It likes to conserve energy and do the things it knows how to do.

The truth is (if you're willing to admit it), not everything is perfect in the Comfort Zone. Perhaps you're always struggling to make ends meet, you don't have the business/career of your dreams, or you're underpaid and giving away your services, whatever the case may be for you at the time.

But what if you're like Jane and want more? Whether it's a higher income, new opportunities, or new connections, there will always be a risk. Sometimes it will work, and sometimes it won't. However, one thing I can promise you is that things will never change if you don't do anything differently.

I've said this before and will continue saying it: You're either growing or dying. You don't stay the same. If you want to grow professionally and personally, and you don't go through the Freak-out Zone, you are not dreaming big enough.

In Jane's coaching sessions, I helped her become more comfortable with expanding who she is and how she presents herself in the world. She learned how to ask for her new pricing with more confidence, and she understood why she was worthy. She didn't realize that before she wasn't showing up in her brilliance, so naturally people weren't willing to pay her more.

YOU ARE ABOUT TO ENTER THE FREAK-OUT ZONE

Here are some signals you are entering the Freak-out Zone:

- » bursts of anger
- » quiet, introspective thoughts
- » restlessness, difficulty sleeping
- » pulling the covers over your head
- » feeling scared, disappointed, or frustrated
- » crying
- » rationalizing going back to your Comfort Zone
- » comparing yourself to others
- » stress and overwhelm
- » looking for the first sign of failure as a reason to go backward

Sometimes, you'll get fooled by your fear during the Freak-out Zone, which was the case with my client Angela. She had been working with me for a few years and had increased her salary to well over six figures. Her husband had a successful career in management, making multi-six-figures. Like most couples, they lived up to their income level. Then Angela's husband's company was sold, and he lost his job. At first, they thought it would be short term, but it lasted months longer than expected. It became difficult to pay their bills on one income.

I remember how proudly she told me that she was getting rid of cable television, dropping out of a class she was taking, and other money-saving changes. If you've ever worked with me or heard me speak, you know I can be direct. When Angela told me what she had done, I said "STOP!" I must have shocked her, which was quite important at this time.

When people's income level unexpectedly drops, they tend to see what they can eliminate. Cable television always seems to be a favorite. There's a problem when you get rid of things from a place of desperation: You start to make yourself smaller and smaller. You constrict and contract. You give up.

What you want to do instead (and this is where the Laws of Attraction come in) is to expand and make yourself bigger. When you're constricting, you're not allowing abundance to come in. On the flip side, when you're expanding, you're opening yourself for more. Imagine if you were to open your arms wide and say, "Here I am. I'm ready to receive abundance." That's much more powerful than contracting and closing yourself off.

Angela's first response was disbelief. Then she got it and had a lightbulb moment. Her energy went from despair to excitement. We strategized additional ways to bring in money, and she left our call ready to go. To pay the bills that were due, she needed over $10,000 within two weeks. In less than that amount of time, she earned $14,000. Interesting how things work when you change your mindset.

Angela's husband also found his dream job a few weeks later. I wasn't surprised to hear her husband's good news. Her good energy was contagious, and he started feeling more uplifted and excited. His newfound confidence was much more attractive to a hiring manager than someone who was scared.

As you can see, Angela had been in her Freak-out Zone and started handling things from a place of fear. When she learned to handle the situation from a place of power, everything changed for her.

The place where most people fail is that they don't like the uncomfortable feeling of the Freak-out Zone. I compare it to being pulled through a keyhole. Things just don't feel normal. However, with the guidance of my coaches, I always come out on the other side at my new level. It's the same with my clients. Often, they go through this phase frightened and scared, yet they are eternally grateful for the transformations that happen.

One of my clients, Beth, wanted to hone in on her niche and marketing message, as she had a big year coming up and needed this done. This is not a split-second process, as it takes time to do it right. Beth was not happy doing the work initially because she needed to be extremely specific and the homework I gave her was extensive. However, over time, her annoyance turned to delight, as she found her blogs and social media posts easier to write, and her video content coming more naturally to her. The response and engagement from this newly expanded online community was overwhelmingly favorable.

I can't begin to tell you how many times Beth previously had the attitude of "Why bother, this is too hard." That's because it was new and would have been easier for her to stay where she was. However, the results were tenfold of what she expected, and she's happy and thriving in her new level of business.

MOST PEOPLE QUIT

Most people give up partly through the Freak-out process. Whether it's the process of finding a new job, decluttering, creating a new program, generating a new financial plan, building a team, finding a romantic partner, or losing weight, most end up quitting. Your mind's natural inclination is to keep you safe. It views safety as something you've done before and knows the outcome. Growth will only happen when you're willing to try something new.

Next time you're scared about being in the Freak-out Zone, I suggest that you celebrate. The only way to avoid the Freak-out Zone is to not dream big enough. Entering this zone means if you stick with it and get the appropriate guidance to support you through to the other side, you will be amazed at the results you get—more than you ever expected!

YOUR BADGE OF HONOR

There are two areas to watch out for in the Freak-out Zone: perfectionism and procrastination. These two often go hand in hand.

Many people walk around wearing perfectionism as if it's a badge of honor. They are so proud of doing things perfectly. Remember getting a gold star on your homework when you were very young? As a child (and even as adults), we all have a fundamental need to be loved and appreciated. Often in my life I was also mistakenly focused on getting that gold star.

Many clients I've worked with are continually striving for that gold star, even as adults. What's interesting is that everyone has a different frame of reference for what perfect looks like.

You could cook a delicious dinner, and someone may declare it perfect, while another might say it's too spicy and yet another, too bland. You can't please everyone. Trying to do so holds back your brilliance.

Four Reasons for Procrastination

I had the honor and privilege of being interviewed to speak on the topic of procrastination for a big online telesummit with over 500,000 listeners.

People procrastinate for four main reasons:

1. *You don't know how to do it.* This goes back to the first step in the Money Acceleration System™: the Comfort Zone. Many people are uncomfortable asking for help and don't know where to get it. Instead of asking for the support they need, they just don't do it. Often, they feel that asking for help is a sign of weakness or will make them look foolish. They think that their question is so big or complicated (or they're the only one with this problem) that there must not be an answer. However, according to the Laws of Attraction, if there's a question, there must be an answer. Ask. You may not know the answer, but someone else will. Most people let not knowing the "how" become a big obstacle.

   There's also that old joke about driving around for hours and not asking for directions. It's up to you how long you want to drive around for when you're lost.

2. *You want someone else to do it for you.* Have you ever seen a parent continually nag their child to clean up their toys? They might ask that child a million times, but it still doesn't get done. It's almost as if that child has selective hearing. Maybe the parent gets angry with the child or even threatens punishment. That may work. However, let's say the parent is expecting company in an hour. When their child doesn't act fast

enough, the parent often will clean the room themselves. The child now knows that if they don't do it, someone else will. Procrastination wins for them!

Have you ever worked with a co-worker who didn't get things done on time, and you ended up picking up the slack? Just like the child, that person sees value in procrastinating, because they know someone else will do their work.

3. *You fear failing.* What happens when things don't work out the way you'd like? You may think you're stupid, or a loser, but the truth is that you usually survive failing. In fact, most of our well-known geniuses failed hundreds of times before a successful invention. Interestingly enough, people are more afraid of the possibility of failing than actually failing. Think about that for a moment. They are willing to hold off taking action, as that fear is so intense.

    This also includes the fear of making a wrong decision. Have you ever met someone who can't make a decision? They might need to ask every person they know for their opinion. They might also spend endless time online researching or shopping. Think about the person who has to test-drive 20 cars or visit open houses for a year before they can make a decision. Somewhere along the line, they lost confidence in their decision-making, and as a result, they now hold off as long as possible. Often, when waiting too long to decide, you lose out on a big opportunity. Perhaps you've heard the expression: "When you snooze, you lose!"

4. *You fear succeeding.* You'd think that no one would be afraid to be successful, but it happens more often than you realize. One reason may be that to be successful, you think someone else will lose. In other words, if you raise your pricing, your clients will be mad. Or if you take the job, someone else won't get it.

    Another reason, which I mentioned previously, is the fear that once you become successful, you will no longer belong to your family or community. You have an unspoken vow to act and behave like them. If you change, they won't like you. You believe that others will resent you for your newfound success.

You may also not see yourself as that successful person (whatever that looks like), and that scares you. If you lose that weight, you'll become too desirable. If you make too much money, everyone will want it. As you can see, this list can go on and on of why a fear of success could hold you back.

When Procrastination Is a Problem

Everyone procrastinates at various times. It becomes a problem when the lack of action stops you from getting what you want or living the life you desire. For example, if you have a pile of magazines on a table and it's messy but doesn't bother you, then not taking the time to straighten up isn't a big deal.

However, if you're looking for a new job and you hesitate to make calls or finish your resume, that's a problem. If people owe you money and you don't take action to get it from them, that becomes a problem. If you have clients/a boss/employees who call you at night and on weekends with little disregard for your time off, and you don't have a conversation regarding these disruptions, that's a problem.

Take a few minutes to learn where procrastination is hurting you by filling out the Procrastination Block Cost Chart™. List the items and the dollar amounts you are losing by not taking action.

PROCRASTINATION BLOCK COST CHART™

	Item	Cost
1.		$
2.		
3.		
4.		
5.		
6.		
7.		
8.		
9.		
10.		
11.		
12.		
13.		
14.		
15.		
16.		
17.		
18.		
19.		
20.		
Total Cost of Procrastination		$

The Cost of Procrastination

Were you surprised by how much procrastination is costing you? Prioritize each of the items and create a plan to take action.

One of my clients, Wendy, was trying to create a big six-month program to offer her clients. She had been working on it for months before our meeting, to no avail. She even told me that her clients were requesting she put this together. When I got to the bottom of why Wendy hadn't finished, her reason was that she feared it wouldn't be good enough.

I was able to help Wendy understand that it was more important for her to help people than wait until her program was perfect. The result? She was able to proceed and enroll many new clients.

Another client, Bonnie, worked at a full-time job and had started a business on the side. She had some clients, and her goal was to leave her full-time job once her side business was bringing in enough income. Bonnie was putting off promoting her business. For example, she had put off building a website. Bonnie reasoned that when she looked at other successful entrepreneurs' websites, they looked great, and her version didn't look anything like them.

I shared with Bonnie that my website was my fifth version and looked nothing like my original. I was willing to bet the same was true with the entrepreneurs she mentioned. Bonnie's mindset work was learning to not compare herself to others, as that would always hold her back. Instead, she needed to learn to swim in her own lane. As a result, she became aware of other areas in her life where she was procrastinating, such as putting out a regular newsletter and networking. I ran into Bonnie recently and not only is she a full-time entrepreneur, but she's also now traveling and speaking to various industry groups.

Who's Perfect?

Occasionally, someone will email me and tell me that they found a typo in something I wrote. Years ago, I used to get upset when someone pointed out an error I had made. Now, I realize I'm human. I will make errors. In fact, the more I do and the more things I try, the more mistakes I will probably make. That's part of the journey. I'd rather make an error than stay stuck and not more forward.

Once, a woman wrote me saying that she could never work with someone who had a typo. That was good news for me, as she probably wasn't my ideal client. When I was a flight attendant and had less-than-perfect passengers on the plane, I learned how not to get annoyed. I reminded myself that I only have them for a few hours, but someone else has to live with them. Now, I bless people who annoy me and give them to The Universe.

I realize there isn't anything that's perfect, except for nature. Everything else is perfectly imperfect or imperfectly perfect. Or as my Mom says, "There is no such thing as a perfect world."

A Fortune 1000 company I was once employed with took the entire group out for a team-building exercise. During this day-long retreat, I learned that "good enough is good enough."

You are good enough! You are brilliant. Go!

Now, let's move even deeper into your Zone of Brilliance in the next chapter.

Lessons in Brilliance

+ If you want to grow to the next level, you must be willing to go through the Freak-out Zone. Most people will turn around and run back to their Comfort Zone rather than risk the uncomfortableness. To make the process go as smoothly and easily as possible, get the guidance of a mentor or coach.

+ You can either be in expansion mode or constriction mode. You can't be in constriction and expect expansion at the same time. It doesn't work that way.

+ Celebrate the Freak-out Zone. As being in the Freak-out Zone is uncomfortable, your natural inclination will be to try to leave. Be aware of what you are going through, and it will make the process less painful. My clients often say to me: "Kate, I know I'm going through the Freak-out Zone," then they laugh. It makes the process more tolerable.

+ Sometimes you won't be aware when you are in the Freak-out Zone. Every now and then, one of my coaches will say something, and I'll realize I'm going through the Freak-out Zone. That creates

a big sigh of relief and gratitude that I have a mentor to guide me
through.

✦ Procrastination and perfectionism are two big potential problems
that happen during this time. Everyone procrastinates at one time
or another. It's when you realize it's holding you back that it's
time to get help.

✦ As everyone has different standards of what perfect is, it's critical
to learn to let go of that goal to be perfect. Releasing that false
measure will make it easier for you to soar.

✦ Fill out the Procrastination Block Chart™. How much is procrastination costing you each year? Make a plan to release the biggest
culprits.

▶ **Don't Get Hijacked!** If you aren't willing to go through the
Freak-out Zone, you will forever be stuck. Review your vision statement and get the support needed. Life is glorious on the other side!

A second warning: Move past inaction. As one pilot told me,
it's all about making a decision based on the best information you
have at the time.

7

Put the Oxygen Mask on Yourself First

So far, I've focused on your inner game—your mindset and the actions you need to take. Now, it's time to look at your outer world and how that affects your success, abundance, and happiness.

I attended one personal development event in a major hotel recently where the floor was bouncing from 1,500 attendees jumping up and down. A few times, I thought our floor was going to collapse beneath us—the vibration was that strong. Everyone was ready to rock their world. When I went home and later connected with some of these people, they were still doing the same old stuff. Nothing had changed for them. Why is that?

You either have an environment that is pulling you forward or holding you back. For you to enter your Zone of Brilliance and remain there, you need a supportive, nurturing environment.

1. YOU FIRST

When I was a flight attendant, there was a common phrase used, and it's still prevalent today: Put the oxygen mask on yourself first. Here's the reason behind its importance. If you're traveling on a plane with a tiny child and you put the mask on the child first, they can't put the mask on you if required to do so in return. They just wouldn't be able to help you. As a result, you might die.

However, if you put the mask on yourself first, you'll then be able to help and assist everyone else around who needs it. That's critical, especially in life-or-death situations.

How often do you take care of others' needs before yourself, whether it's with food, medical care, purchases, or giving your time? It might be great that you run errands for a neighbor, but at what cost to you? If you don't make time for yourself to do what you love, eventually, you'll feel empty and possibly resentful. When you take care of yourself first and go to that yoga class (or whatever lights you up), you'll be a more exciting partner, more energized parent, and a happier person. Taking care of you first adds fuel to all the other things you need to do in your life.

When my client Elisa wanted to grow her 3-year-old business, she was at a loss where to start. She was married and had several adult children. Her entire life had been all about taking care of her family. She cooked, cleaned, and made sure her family had all they needed. Now that the children were out of the house, she had the time to earn additional income to improve her family's lifestyle.

I asked her several serious questions about what she wanted her business to look like and who her ideal clients were. Elisa couldn't answer. She honestly didn't know. For the past 20 years, her life had been about taking care of others. She had forgotten to think about what she wanted and what made her happy. That was a huge "aha" moment for her and the beginning of her journey to building a successful business.

Before you sit there and think that I'm talking about being selfish, I'm not. I'm referring to taking care of yourself. The happier and healthier you are, the more you have to give. You're ultimately the person

Taking Care of You

Take a few minutes to reflect on your days and write your responses in your journal:

1. When do you take time for just you—to do something that makes you happy?
2. What things are you doing for yourself daily?
3. How often do you give up your needs to make someone else happy?

Assess your answers. What do you want to change? Go or Don't Go. It's your choice.

responsible for you—no one else. If you don't take good care of you, who will?

2. MEDIA

I used to have a few televisions in my home, including one in my bedroom. I had gotten into the habit of falling asleep watching television in my corporate days. Once, on vacation, I stayed at this lovely resort on the ocean. The room was gorgeous, but there was one thing missing: There wasn't a television. I had never experienced that before, as I was used to a television providing background noise. It was quite an adjustment to learn to be OK with the quiet and to fall asleep that way, but I learned how during my 10-day vacation there.

When I returned home, the first thing I did was to get rid of the television in my bedroom. I've since noticed that instead of waking up in the middle of the night, I now have a restful eight hours of sleep.

I learned later through my studies and education that what we're exposed to for the last few hours before we go to sleep affects the type of rest we have and how we wake up in the morning. Have you noticed that if you go to sleep worrying about something, when you wake up that's the first thing on your mind? That's not good, and it prevents a restful sleep.

If you want to get your best chance at a good night's sleep, in the two hours before going to bed:

» don't watch violent or scary television shows.
» don't watch the news.
» don't watch/read/listen to anything potentially upsetting on television or social media.

A few hours before going to sleep, you want to prime your brain to start to relax. At this point, you should be doing things that calm and soothe you. That could be listening to music, meditation, or whatever you find relaxing. You'll notice a significant improvement in your sleep. That's important because you want to start your morning off with energy, not feeling sluggish, as if you need a huge cup of coffee to get moving.

3. YOUR PHYSICAL ENVIRONMENT

No matter how upbeat and positive you are, if you go home to a place you hate, your energy, productivity, and happiness will be affected. If this sounds like you, a great place to start is by decluttering your home and not tolerating items that need to be repaired.

Declutter Your Home

One of my favorite things about staying at a hotel is how clean the room looks. You won't find a lot of items lying on surfaces and taking up space. I love that feeling of vastness.

Several times a year I host the Money Acceleration Retreat™ for a small, exclusive group to work on significant breakthroughs in their life and work. I also love to attend retreats myself. Returning home from one that I attended, I realized that for me to implement the changes that were taught, I needed my home to match my new mindset. I decided to declutter my entire home, which was not an easy task. I made it a priority, and as I worked through different areas, I started getting excited about all the stuff I was getting rid of. I could finally see what I owned. I felt a lot of pride being able to give, donate, or throw away over 60 huge bags of belongings. Nothing that I eliminated has been missed since then.

More recently, I did another decluttering project in my home, this time taking it a step further. The experience was transformative on two levels. First, I realized where I was spending money based on what I was getting rid of. I saw where the waste was. Second, my heart felt so full thinking about all the people who could use the clothes I was donating. They were all in beautiful condition; some even had their original tags. I envisioned that these clothes, which were sitting in my closet taking up space, might help someone get their dream job. I can't even begin to tell you how good that felt. The thought of decluttering and organizing can sometimes feel overwhelming, but honestly, the results are worth it.

Here are a few suggestions to make it go easier:

» *Divide your home into sections and work on the area that bothers you the most first.* I like to conquer the biggest offender right off the bat. However, you can also start with a small area that you can quickly finish, which will give you the feeling of achievement and encourage you to do more.

» *Take everything out of the drawers, closets, cabinets, and shelves.* When I put all the coats and jackets I owned on top of my bed, I was in shock by how much I had. So many had been hidden in the closet. When you're able to see everything in a specific category, it makes it easier to decide what you want to keep or eliminate.

» *Look at each item.* If you don't love it, get rid of it, even if it's never been used.

» *Try putting an item in a box/bag and off to the corner if you're afraid to get rid of it because you think you might need it.* If you don't use it in a month, get rid of it. If it's something that holds personal value, take a picture of it. It won't take up physical space, yet you won't lose the memory.

Once you finish decluttering, you will feel so good with how your home looks. I felt like I had moved into a new home, which was energizing.

Stop Tolerating Items that Need Repairing
In your Comfort Zone, it becomes easy to overlook and ignore the things that don't make you happy. Maybe it's a dish with a chip, a loose button falling off, a door that needs repair, or a drawer stuffed shut. Whatever it might be, even though you might not be regularly mentioning it, you still pick up on the fact that they are there and it annoys you. I had one bathroom drawer that had an acrylic container inside it that never shut right. Every time I opened that drawer, I silently cursed it. Finally, I bought a new container that fit perfectly, and I haven't thought about it since. Why get annoyed every day over the small things? Use the following Toleration Chart to deal with it.

TOLERATION CHART

1. _____
   _____

2. _____
   _____

3. _____
   _____

4. _____
   _____

5. _____
   _____

6. _____
   _____

7. _____
   _____

8. _____
   _____

9. _____
   _____

10. _____
    _____

» Fill in your tolerations.
» Now, go back and prioritize your list. What is the most important thing to fix first? It doesn't matter if it's the biggest or small-
est—it's the one that annoys you the most.
» Create an action plan and deadline to repair the first problem
on your list.
» Repeat this process for all the items on the list.

4. COMMUNITY

To stay on track and live your best life, you need a community that
supports you. This can include romantic relationships, partners, family, friends, business associates, coaches, mentors, team members,
employees, and neighbors.

Don't fall into the trap of (and I used to be guilty of this) sharing
your dreams and goals with people who won't (or don't) support you.
Their lack of support can show up in many ways.

Sometimes, it's deliberate; other times it's not. Sometimes they
"just don't want you to get hurt," so they try to stop you from doing
something. Maybe it didn't work for them or others they know, so they
trying to "save" you from getting hurt, too. Other times, they're afraid
you'll become too successful and leave them. Sometimes they're jeal-
ous; sometimes they just don't care.

This becomes a big problem when someone pops a big hole in a
dream you shared. When one of my clients told her friend about a trip
she was planning, her friend replied, "I would never in a million years
want to go there!" My client left the conversation feeling sad and
worried—perhaps she had made the wrong vacation decision. She
hadn't! Her mistake was sharing something important with someone
who wasn't in her inner circle. Refer to the following diagram to learn
who's in your sphere of influence and who you can trust to share private information with.

BRILLIANT INNER CIRCLE DIAGRAM™

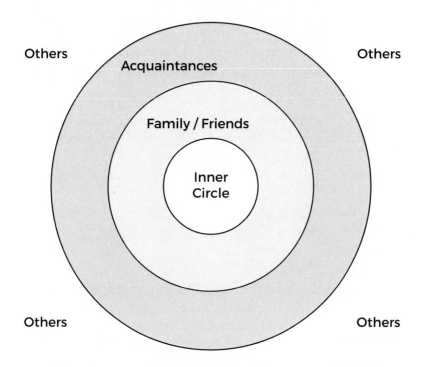

» *Inner circle*: These are the people you can say anything to. They understand you and are happy for you. They don't judge you and will always support you. You may find you only have one or two people in here. Sometimes, clients tell me initially that no one is in their inner circle, so they need to find the right person/people to fill it.

» *Friends and family:* These are people who know you pretty well and vice versa. Some may have known you your entire life. The problem is that there is often a lot of baggage with these people, and it can be hard to get their full support, especially if you're trying to make a huge change in your life. Your change may make them uncomfortable, as they only know you in a certain way.

» *Acquaintances:* This includes people you see periodically, like co-workers. You both smile and ask how the other is doing. These are surface conversations, and you really don't know much about what the other person thinks and believes. You don't typically share that type of personal information.

» *Others:* These are the people you come in contact with over time. It could be the cashier at the grocery store, or the person on the other end of the 1-800 customer service line, or the person staffing the tollbooth. You both tell each other to have a nice day.

Notice that starting from the outside ring, each circle gets smaller and smaller, as the exclusivity factor increases. Your inner circle is the most exclusive of them all.

Sometimes people move in and out of the various categories. Someone can start as a co-worker and become your best friend. Or you may have a sibling whom you shared every secret with during childhood, but as you got older, your lives took different paths and you went in your own directions.

As one of my clients describes it, you want to be careful who you allow into your country club. In other words, you should always evaluate who's in your inner circle and whether you want to renew their membership. If someone in your inner circle is going through a busy time, you may want to shift them into a different category until their relationship with you becomes a priority again. It can also work in the opposite direction—moving someone from an outer circle into your inner circle, as your relationship with them improves.

Who's in Your Country Club?

It's so important to recognize who is and isn't a member, as you don't want to be sharing your most personal information with the wrong people. I see this often when getting my nails and hair done. People will share the most intimate details of their life with a virtual stranger. You don't want your bubble burst. Think about who you choose to tell something to before you tell it.

When I see people being coached by their friends or people at their level, it always seems like the blind leading the blind. How can someone help you who has never done it before? It doesn't make sense, does it?

Have you ever been advised that if you want to improve your tennis game, you should play with those who are better than you? It's the same with your work. Hang out with those who are achieving the success you'd like to achieve. Some people believe that your income is the average of the five people you associate with.

THE BRILLIANT COUNTRY CLUB CHART™

1. Mentors/Teachers

   _____   _____

   _____   _____

   _____   _____

2. Cheerleaders/Supporters

   _____   _____

   _____   _____

   _____   _____

3. Confidants

   _____   _____

   _____   _____

   _____   _____

4. Role Models

   _____   _____

   _____   _____

   _____   _____

5. Naysayers

   _____   _____

   _____   _____

   _____   _____

I want things to be better for you, so look at your community. Start by filling out the Brilliant Country Club Chart™.

» *Mentors/Teachers:* These are the people who guide you to show up in your brilliance.
» *Cheerleaders/Supporters:* They're always on your side, encouraging you to move forward.
» *Confidants:* You can tell them anything. They won't judge, and they can keep a secret.
» *Role Models:* These are the people you look up to, whether you know them personally or admire them from afar.
» *Naysayers*: They will try to burst your bubble with all the reasons why you can't or won't be successful.

Any surprises about who was on your list?

True Confessions

I need to confess something. Things haven't always come easily for me. When I started my business, it was without any support. My friends didn't get it, as they wanted me to stay in the industry. My family probably thought I was crazy and kept suggesting that I continue my job hunt. The only person who believed in me was me. Against all odds, I made my business work. Later, my parents were full of pride and excitement with all I was doing. I believe they were just scared of the big risk I was taking. I knew I had more to lose by not taking it.

5. HEALTH

Straight out, I will tell you I'm not a health expert. However, I've noticed (as have my clients) an improved health and mindset when you pay attention to what you eat and drink. I've given up caffeine and meat, and do my best to avoid sugar. Find out what foods make you feel happier and more energetic, and stick to them. The ones that make you feel sluggish, tired, uncomfortable, reduce or eliminate them from your diet. Exercise regularly, whether it's going to a gym, out for a walk or run, or doing yoga, Pilates, or tai chi—you choose. Frequently schedule anything that puts your body into motion and makes you feel happy.

6. APPEARANCE

When I was a flight attendant, there was a woman in my training class who was fired because she wouldn't put lipstick on for class after lunch. Truthfully, it wasn't as simple as that, as she did give the instructor a bit of a hard time, saying she had already put lipstick on that day. You might think that's kind of harsh.

However, I will tell you that when you feel good about how you look, you will have more confidence. More confidence leads to more energy, taking more risks, trying new things, and attracting more success (clients, opportunities, money, and more) into your life. I'm not saying to go out and buy a designer wardrobe or be superficial. I'm saying to show pride in how you present yourself, even if it's only for you. You matter.

Whether you have a new or old car, wash it and keep it clean. Whether you live in a studio or mansion, be proud of how it looks. Brush your teeth after eating to keep your smile beautiful.

7. MOVEMENT

As a business owner or professional, you probably spend more time in front of the computer than you're even aware. If you don't have an ergonomic setup for your chair and computer, most likely at some point you will end up with various health issues. Take preventive care by setting up a healthy work area.

Also, at least once an hour, get up from your chair and stretch and move. Physically, this will keep you limber and is good for your body. For your creativity, there are huge benefits, as your mind needs to take regular breaks and refuel. Be kind to your mind and take frequent relaxation breaks. You may even want to set a timer for at least once every hour as a reminder.

8. UNCONDITIONAL LOVE

Numerous studies prove that having a pet makes you happier. If you follow me on Facebook, you know how much my cairn terrier, Cali, means to me. That 17-pound dog has changed my life for the better. She has been with me through thick and thin. Whether I am making money or not, she always loves me. Whenever I return home, she always wags her tail, and it doesn't matter if I've been gone for five minutes or five hours.

If you're not a pet lover, get a plant. If you're not a plant lover, bring in flowers. These are things that will help you enjoy every day.

9. SUNLIGHT

Many people find their emotions changing when there is less daylight. If you're one of them, find ways to increase your sunshine in the winter, whether it's buying certain lights, traveling during the winter to sunny locales, or even moving to a new location. One of my clients hated winter so much that her dream was to move to Florida within the year. I got her in action so that when she moved later that year, she already had a list of clients.

Everything is energy. When you take the time to care about how you live, you will see the results in other areas of your life, too.

Your physical environment affects how you think, feel, and act. This applies to your home and (home) office. If your environment doesn't change, you can't. Look around, take action, and be good to yourself.

Ask for what you need. As my Mother taught me: "You don't ask, you don't get." That training from her has been like a superpower, allowing me to live my best life. That phrase felt like I was given the keys to the castle, and in thousands of times during my life, it has empowered me and changed the results for the better.

When I was a teenager, I occasionally babysat for a neighbor who was the president of a very prestigious college in Boston. One time, they contacted me to babysit, and before I could say yes, my Mother reminded me that they hadn't paid me for the previous time. She said I had two options: Either don't say anything and not get paid, or remind them they owed me money. For a teenager, this was a big step. I had to learn to get out of my Comfort Zone and ask this president for payment due. It was scary, and I did it. I got paid, and going forward they always paid me on time.

Recently, at an event I attended, one of the attendees complained she had noisy neighbors. She didn't want to ask the front desk to change her room, as it would have been too much trouble. Instead, she moaned and groaned about her neighbors every morning. If that had been me, I would have had no problem immediately asking for a different room, as I require a good night's sleep to function optimally throughout the day.

I challenge you to make one change today. What's it going to be? Start small. Small steps lead to bigger steps.

In the next chapter, you'll learn how to break through your glass ceiling and stop those paralyzing patterns.

Lessons in Brilliance

✦ Put the oxygen mask on yourself first. The better you take care of yourself, the more you will have to give to others.

✦ Your environment is either pulling your forward or holding you back. Be discerning of what you allow in your home. If you don't love it, get rid of it.

✦ Choose your confidants carefully. You want people who support you, not burst your bubble.

✦ Add things to your life that make you feel good and energized. Eliminate the others.

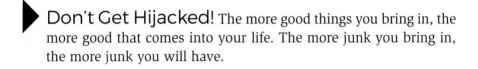 **Don't Get Hijacked!** The more good things you bring in, the more good that comes into your life. The more junk you bring in, the more junk you will have.

8

Breaking Through Your Glass Ceiling

During the first year of my business, my Dad and I would always have multiple conversations about how things were going. He wanted to know if I was making money. After all, being a good Dad, he wanted to know I was doing well. I'll never forget one time when I answered the question for him, and he said, "I knew that would be the answer."

I looked at him and asked, "What do you mean?" After all, my Dad was super-smart, but as far as I knew, he wasn't a fortuneteller.

He replied that every third month, I didn't make money. I was horrified. Was he right? I didn't want to believe him. When I arrived home, I pulled up my records, and sure enough, he was correct. One month I'd earn money, the next I'd earn more money, but on the third month, my income would drop. The first time that happened, I blamed it on the time of year, figuring everyone was away for the summer and they didn't need coaching. On the fourth month, my income started to rise again, as it did in the fifth month. However, in the sixth month, it dropped again. I figured it was because it was the holiday season and no one needed coaching. In the seventh and eighth months, it went back up. Can you see the pattern? I sure didn't, until my Dad pointed it out. Once I realized I was in a pattern, I had two choices: either to live with it or change it. Go or Don't Go!

I opted to change it and knew enough that I couldn't change this pattern myself. I hired coaches: one to help me with the business side and the other for mindset, since I couldn't find a coach with a high level of expertise in both areas.

The business coach helped me create higher-level coaching programs and attract clients to fill them. The mindset coach helped uncover a big block that had been holding me back. When I had started my business, it was during the horrible recession in the United States. My friends were continuing to lose their jobs. I hadn't realized that every time I started to make money, I had a subconscious belief pop up that "who was I to make a lot of money in this economy when my friends were losing their jobs?" For some reason, I was feeling guilty about my success. My coach helped me realize that my success had absolutely nothing to do with their job loss. As I understood that new belief deep in my subconscious mind, my income accelerated and that horrible pattern of "good month/bad month" disappeared.

Your limited and core beliefs will always hold back your income. I could tell you hundreds of stories about this pattern, and I'll share another one with you later that happened to a client of mine.

Are you starting to think of a pattern you might have? If so, one of the most important things is to first figure out what you want that next level to look like. Take a few minutes to answer these questions honestly:

1. What is the next level:
   » in your business or career?
   » in your life?
   » in your bank account?
   » for your relationships, family, and friends?
   » with your community?
   » for your legacy?
2. What fears, doubts, beliefs, and stories do you think are holding you back?
3. What lack of knowledge is keeping you stuck?

Were you surprised by any of the answers you wrote?

Now that you know what the next level is you're targeting, let's talk about how a good month/bad month game can show up in your life. Note that I will be using money as the example. However, you can replace it with other goals, such as weight loss, career promotions, and so on. Now, take out your journal and fill in the numbers in my BRILLIANCE Breakthrough Formula™:

1. Goal:
2. Most Earned:
3. Amount Needed:
4. Survival Number:

Let's go over each line of my formula in detail:

1. *What is your income goal per month?* This is what I call your imagination number—the one you believe would allow you to live a cool lifestyle where you could do what you wanted to do.
2. *What is the greatest amount of money you've earned per month?* You want to earn more money than you've made in the past, so this number gives you a benchmark, a target to surpass.
3. *How much money do you need to receive each month?* This is the amount that will pay your bills for your current lifestyle. For example, rent/mortgage, car payments, groceries, dining out, shopping, insurance, coaching services, and so on.
4. *What is your survival number?* This is the number everyone hates to admit they know. It's the number that, when worse comes to worst, you absolutely must have to live. It's your minimum amount. You're taking the third number and eliminating all the extras, like dining out and movies, and only leaving the necessities.

Here's an example of what the formula looks like when it's filled in.

BRILLIANCE Breakthrough Formula™
1. **Goal:** $10,000/month
2. **Most Earned:** $7,000/month
3. **Amount Needed:** $5,000/month
4. **Survival Number:** $2,000/month

Most people's incomes will average around the amount needed. It's their Comfort Zone. When they start making more money, it brings up a lot of fears, doubts, beliefs, and stories about who they are and whether they deserve this. You must have the self-image of a person at that new level. You also must know how to make it happen. Most lottery ticket winners lose their money within a few years because they don't see themselves as millionaires. Many had been hourly workers that bought tickets week after week for years until they finally won. They still see themselves as hourly workers. They don't know how to live like a millionaire or manage that amount of money. Their income ends up dropping to where they are comfortable. If you've ever lost weight and gained it back, it's the same story. You don't see yourself as a thin, fit person. In the previous example of my story, I didn't believe I deserved to make that much money due to the economy, so I didn't have the mindset to go along with that increased wealth. Also, I lacked some of the marketing strategies to help get and keep me at that new income level.

On the flip side, let's say your income drops. Maybe you have a family or medical emergency. What most people do is eliminate all excess. As I mentioned in Chapter 6, doing so makes you constrict and contract and doesn't allow for more abundance to come in. According to Parkinson's Law, people will use as much time as they have been given to complete an assignment. Regarding money and that law, people live up to their income and will spend as much money as they earn. Therefore, if you reduce your monthly bills from $5,000 to $3,000, and you're like most people, you won't end up with an additional $2,000. Either you'll find somewhere else to spend that money, or you'll notice your income dropping to match that new number. I remember when I quit smoking, everyone said: "Think about all of the extra money you'll have now that you're not buying cigarettes." It never happened. I have yet to meet a former smoker who ended up with extra money. People tend to spend what they have.

Back to the BRILLIANCE Breakthrough Formula™. It's dangerous to lower your expenses without carefully thinking things through. Instead, you need find ways to increase your revenue.

SISTERLY LOVE

As an owner of a marketing company, Donna couldn't understand why her 5-year-old business wasn't able to cross over the six-figure mark. When she became my client, she told me that her clients loved her work, but it seemed that whenever she would sign on a new client and get ready to do her happy dance, an existing client would put her services on hold. She was playing her version of good month/bad month.

Donna told me that growing up, she was always responsible for her younger brother. She remembered being 6 years old and her Mom asking if Joey was OK—"Did Joey have his turn?" "Did Joey need anything?" This was because he was slightly physically disabled, and it took him longer to accomplish tasks than his sister. She always needed to be on the lookout for him to make sure he was taken care of. Fast-forward years later. She's now in her mid-40s, and Joey is a few years younger. Interestingly enough, they both became business owners. Where Donna's business was thriving, his wasn't doing very good.

What I uncovered is that her subconscious mind still believed that she needed to wait for Joey. She couldn't have success until Joey did. It's interesting how our minds work! When I helped her release that belief that she needed to wait for him, her business took off in a flash. Soon after, she happily reported being on track to make a quarter of a million dollars that year.

Another one of my clients, Ellen, was also on the verge of six figures but couldn't cross over. She was sick and tired of playing the good month/bad month game. After lots of probing questions, Ellen shared with me that growing up, she had been a Daddy's girl. She and her father always spent lots of special time together. She remembered that he got a new job as a CEO of a Fortune 500 company. There was a lot of excitement going on in her family at that time due to his new position, increased salary, and so on. So much so that they had a big celebration party for her father to honor his new success.

After he started his job, he traveled quite a bit. When he was home, he was stressed out and short-tempered, and complained about clients and employees. Generally, he always seemed unhappy. He never seemed to have time for his precious little daughter, Ellen, anymore.

I uncovered that Ellen's young mind formed a belief that success made people unhappy and mean. Here's where I connected the dots. Many people believe that earning six figures is a magic number and sign of success. Ellen believed that if she earned that much money, she would become unhappy and mean. There was no way she wanted to live her life like that. So, she would subconsciously self-sabotage her income. I was able to help her shift her beliefs around earning six figures, and her income increased. She learned that she could choose how she wanted to act with that new income level. Her father's experience didn't have to be hers. That allowed her to earn multi-six-figures.

Back to the question I asked you earlier: Where are you playing the good month/bad month game in your life? The fabulous thing is that once you understand how to break through, you can do it repeatedly. The first time you might raise your income by $10,000, the next time it might be $15,000, then $25,000, and on and on. There's no stopping on how far you can go.

Being brilliant changes everything, as you'll learn in the next chapter.

Lessons in Brilliance

✦ Take time to answer the questions and determine what your next level will look like. Don't write what you think it should be; write what you want it to be.

✦ Fill out the BRILLIANCE Breakthrough Formula™. Do you remember when it was hard to maintain your highest level of income? Or, on the flip side, when you had to reduce your expenses quickly to get through a troubled time?

✦ When and where have you played the good month/bad month game? Do you see a pattern?

✦ You must have a new image to maintain your new income level. If you still see yourself as a $5,000/month person, you won't be able to remain at the $10,000 level.

✦ A new strategy is required to reach the next level. You will not know how to get there, because it's new to you. That's why it's so important to find and hire additional resources to make the process smoother.

Don't Get Hijacked! It's easy to blame your lack of breaking through on external factors. I did that at the beginning of my business. However, until you accept personal responsibility, you will not be able to break through. Are you ready to do that?

9

Zone of Brilliance

Have you ever had an experience when something popped out of your mouth and you'd look around, wondering who said it? You said it— and it was brilliant! In fact, it was so good, you wished that someone had recorded it so you'd have it forever. The interesting thing is that it just flowed out, and it was perfect. You were in your Zone of Brilliance, which is the last step in my proprietary Money Acceleration System™.

What does "brilliance" mean? Typically, people think it's about being super-smart, and that is part of it, but not in the way you think (although I do tend to attract intelligent people to me). Being brilliant is more about an inner knowing and glow that shines outward. Just like a diamond that sparkles and shines, which attracts people to look at it, being brilliant attracts more abundance to you. You're spending your time on the areas in which you are brilliant, based on what you discovered in the Four Quadrants of Brilliance™.

The Zone of Brilliance is when everything makes sense—your work, business, and personal life. You're doing what you love, and you're respected and appreciated. You're showing up fully as who you are. There are fewer things to worry about and more love to enjoy. You're happy, charismatic, and confident—and it shows!

When my clients are in the Zone of Brilliance, they earn the most money they ever have. They're thoroughly enjoying what they're doing, and surprise, surprise, they are having the most fun!

I've seen the Zone of Brilliance show up over and over in so many ways. Have you ever traveled and had everything go perfectly? Traffic flows, and you get to the airport on time. There are short lines for check-in and through security. Your gate is close by, and there are lots of seats to choose from. The plane is boarded efficiently and quickly, with plenty of room for your carry-on bags. The seat next to you is vacant. The flight takes off right away, it's a smooth trip, and before you know it, you've landed in your destination. Your checked bags are among the first to show up at baggage claim, allowing the person who was meeting you at the airport to park right in front of the exit door. Nice and easy! Don't you love when that happens? You hold the thought that "things are always working out for me." Of course they are—you're brilliant!

When several of my clients have held their own live events, beforehand, they felt so right about everything that they were in complete control. Not in a control-freak way, as it was more from a place of confidence that everything was exactly as it should be. As a result, their events were highly successful.

Another one of my clients, John, wanted to expand on a new venture. His existing business was doing quite well, and we had put in a lot of foundational processes and procedures. His team had also been groomed to step up to their next level, allowing John to join a new project and still have enough income to live on from his primary business.

Truthfully, the new project lit him up more than his current business. However, if he hadn't had everything in place, he wouldn't have been able to move forward. He needed to have the systems, team, income, and time to make this happen. The most important factor was his mindset, as he learned how to believe in himself and what was possible for him.

Sometimes you'll only have moments in your Zone of Brilliance, although my intention is for you to spend more and more time there so it becomes your new normal.

Paul was at his wit's end when he came to work with me. He didn't know what to do. He was stressed about money and specifically about being able to take his three young children to Disney World the next winter. His children had their hearts set on going, but Paul didn't see how it was possible. As a self-employed photographer, he didn't envision enough money coming in. Not being able to take his children on this vacation was breaking his heart. As he didn't know what else to do, he booked a session with me.

During the session, I helped him reduce his stress, come up with ideas to earn more money, and ultimately feel more confident. At the end of our session, Paul (who was a man's man and not an emotional guy) gave me a big huge hug and had tears in his eyes. He told me he hadn't felt that good in 10 years and felt as if a huge weight had been lifted off him. Paul now had a plan for Disney World and beyond. He was in his Zone of Brilliance!

With a little bit of prodding and my guidance, Paul was able to come up with many of these ideas himself. Previously, his stress level had been so impossibly high that he couldn't clear his mind to uncover solutions, and as a result, he didn't believe this dream was possible.

How do you know when you're in your Zone of Brilliance? You will know it without a doubt. Everything seems more natural, thoughts flow, creativity abounds, and your self-confidence is unshakable.

My experience is that everything seems "right." I know how to make the decisions that honor me. I don't need to ask others' opinions or get their approval. Instead, I move forward in the direction I choose at the pace that feels right. Interestingly enough, abundance happens so much faster in this zone, with much less effort. That's one of the reasons I've given you so many exercises within this book to help you get here.

Before my Dad passed away, I was able to be with him and my family in the hospital. Spending those last few days with my Dad was the most impactful time of my life. When he was in a coma and on life support, I felt that he had already transitioned. I held this firm belief that his life, my life, and this experience during his final days had to mean something. The months before, I was in the process of evaluating things in my life. I noticed I was acting on things that no longer made sense for me, so it was time for me to make a big change.

My biggest frustration is that I didn't know what my vision looked like. I couldn't find any role models who were swimming in their lane. I felt that most were following the crowd, and I noticed a high level of lack of integrity. I found that very discouraging, as I so wanted someone to model. No one seemed to have the entire package. Instead, I found the characteristics I was looking for in bits and pieces in others. One leader had one beautiful trait and another was fabulous at something else. I imagined how it would feel to be the person I desired to be and made my decisions from that place. The rest I would figure out as I went along.

When my Dad passed, that propelled me to move at an even faster rate, as I have important work to do in the world. It was time for me to stop making sure everything was right (or perfect) before proceeding. Instead, I launched full steam ahead. I eliminated what no longer felt good to me and focused only on things that honored me.

As a result, not only do I speak nationally, I am also invited to speak on main stages internationally and share my message. The clients I work with are fantastic, and their transformations are fabulous. I have a two-week unplugged Mediterranean vacation planned for later this year, along with several other vacations. My team supports me and has my back. My business is more profitable than ever. I'm thriving, and I feel that those around me are doing the same. I feel happy, proud, confident, excited, loved, safe, grounded, and brilliant.

This zone is when you've learned to trust your inner wisdom— your higher self—to guide you to make the best decisions.

In the Zone of Brilliance, you will still have fears, doubts, beliefs, and old stories. The difference is that now you have the resources to shift and release them, instead of letting them hold you back. You're more aware of what is going on. You understand a thought is just a thought.

How will your Zone of Brilliance show up for you? You'll know because everything makes sense. You'll become a magnet, and due to your level of confidence, you'll attract others. You'll have an inner glow from so much happiness that you won't be able to contain yourself. Enjoy it. You deserve it!

One of my clients recently paid me a high compliment. She said, "Once you go into the Zone of Brilliance with Kate, there is no turning back. You've already been stretched." If you compare that to the metaphor of a rubber band, once it's been stretched, it never returns to its original shape. We'll cover how to ground into your brilliance in the next chapter.

Lessons in Brilliance

+ Being brilliant is an inner knowing and glow that shines outward.
+ When you're in your Zone of Brilliance, everything makes sense. You feel on top of the world.
+ When you're in your Zone of Brilliance, you trust yourself to make decisions and know you have made the right ones.
+ During this time, a great mentor will work with you to help you develop your inner guidance system and learn to listen to it.

▶ **Don't Get Hijacked!** As enjoyable as the Zone of Brilliance is, you can't stay there. Life is a journey. You're either growing or dying—you can't remain static. After you've been at this level for a while, something will catch your eye and you'll want something more. Thus, the process must be repeated, as your Zone of Brilliance has become your Comfort Zone. Go or Don't Go!

10

Staying in Your Zone

Your Zone of Brilliance is always changing as you grow. As a child, you were in your brilliance when you wrote that report, created that science project, or hit that home run. Those were great successes. However, you're not a child anymore. On the flip side, as an adult, you don't stop growing. Many make a mistake and think that they do.

I remember being a flight attendant, age 21 and right out of college. I thought I was so smart and knew everything. At first, when people senior to me tried to teach me things, I believed I knew better and didn't listen. That philosophy didn't serve me and was short-lived.

What I love about how I look at my life now is that it's continuously growing and changing. As good as things are today for me, this is not my end or stopping point.

I tell my private clients that I see great things for them, which I do. When they ask me what, I don't give them a specific answer, as I don't want to project my vision onto theirs. My role is to support their dreams and guide them to success. I believe they are meant for greatness. The fact that they are always looking to grow, expand, learn, and act shows me that they are well on their way.

GETTING GROUNDED

I want to set you up to succeed on your journey to success. The following are rituals, actions, and systems to keep you grounded. Years ago, I never would have known what grounded even meant.

In airline terminology, being grounded isn't a great thing. It means to be stuck, not moving, as in "all flights are grounded due to inclement weather."

However, in our lives, it means something quite different. Here's my definition: Whether something good or bad happens, it doesn't change who I am, my self-worth, or my value. This was one of the biggest and hardest lessons for me to learn. If I didn't have a fantastic coach to work diligently with on this, I would have missed out on so much, and my life would have been much harder. As a result, I am always reinforcing this message with my clients.

If someone says no to one of my clients, I don't want them to feel bad about themselves. If their car breaks, I don't want them to feel life is not supporting them. If their home needs an unexpected repair, I don't want them to feel things are going against them. If there's a problem in their relationship or family, I don't want them to feel less than or not enough.

The reason you have felt this way before is your mind naturally goes into victim mode as you have created this pattern. You play these words over and over again in your head:

» Why does this always happen to me?
» I knew this wouldn't work.
» I just don't have any luck.
» I shouldn't have bothered.
» Things never work out for me.
» Or something along those lines.

When you go into victim mode, you're not brilliant. You can only have one emotion at a time. Either you're a victim, or you're brilliant. You can't be a brilliant victim. It's one or the other. It's your choice. Go or Don't Go!

I recommend using the following seven techniques daily to stay grounded and in your brilliance.

1. Take Personal Responsibility

Own your behavior, thoughts, and actions. Maybe your parents taught you something negative about money. They don't control your mind. You control your own mind. You always have the power to choose and change your thoughts.

If you eat that piece of cake, own the fact that it will make you gain weight. If you don't work out today, own the fact that you're not keeping yourself healthy. If you choose to go to sleep later than usual, own the fact that you will be sleep-deprived the next morning. (Many researchers believe that if you get six hours of sleep or less, your mind functions on the same level as if you were legally drunk!) If you have your own business and don't have a marketing plan to bring in new clients, own that fact when your income doesn't rise.

On the flip side, when you eat healthily, be proud. Own that behavior! When you take consistent action to grow your business, be proud. Own that behavior! When you ask for support to help you in an area you're stuck in, be proud. Own that behavior!

2. Be Proud of Yourself

There are several ways to be proud and own your behavior. When you were little, you might have received a gold star on your forehead or your paperwork. As an adult, no one is going to give you a gold star, so do it yourself. Learn how to be proud of yourself.

- » Literally, you can put a gold star or sticker on your paperwork. I give the members of my coaching group stickers to use as they choose.
- » Keep a journal where you list your daily accomplishments. These won't always be significant, huge results. Sometimes, it's as simple as making your bed, doing the dishes, or holding the door for someone.
- » Immediately after you take an action you're proud of, do a happy dance, clap your hands, or say loudly "woo-hoo." You could even jump up and touch the ceiling—whatever makes you celebrate yourself.

3. Keep a Journal

Maintain a journal that you write in every evening so you wrap up your day feeling good. Some people prefer gratitude journals, where they write several things that they are grateful for. Another option is to write your daily celebrations in your journal. It feels good to remember all that happened during the day, and it reinforces self-pride.

The most important message for you to remember is that you don't have to write about huge items. You only need to understand that your focus brings more of these things into your life. Start small and watch how things grow.

Some days I have to search for something to write about. Other days, my hand gets a cramp writing all that I want. By getting it out of your head and onto a piece of paper, it will reinforce the positive memories in your mind.

It doesn't matter whether you choose the gratitude or celebrations style. Do what feels good. Studies on positivity and happiness have determined that the action of writing uplifting memories every day brings more joy to your life.

4. Say a Daily Word or Mantra

When you find yourself losing focus, getting distracted, or feeling stressed, saying a daily word or mantra helps bring you back to the present. Remember, your fears, doubts, beliefs, and stories aren't real. However, if you believe them, they become real and block success from you.

In the morning, before you begin your day, close your eyes, relax, and ask yourself what word feels important to you today. What characteristic or feeling would you like to guide you? Examples of words my clients have chosen in the past are: permission, focused, powerful, energetic, fearless, and so on.

Here's an easy mantra I learned years ago in that meditation class I took on vacation:

"Breathing in I feel _____. Breathing out I release _____."

Examples of this are:
» Breathing in I feel calm. Breathing out I release stress and overwhelm.
» Breathing in I feel excitement. Breathing out I release chaos.
» Breathing in I feel safe. Breathing out I release fear.

Try it and notice how you feel calmer and more centered when you do this exercise. Repeat each mantra several times throughout your day as needed.

5. Use Affirmations and Power Statements

An affirmation is a positive statement of something that you want to happen. For example, "I easily earn enough money to pay for all I want," "I am earning at least a million dollars from my programs, products, and services," or "My body is healthy, toned, and attractive." Affirmations are usually parts of your vision statement. They remind you of your future goal and what you want to attract into your life.

A power statement is a belief you already have that you need to be reminded of. This means it's something that your conscious mind already believes. These are great to use when you're feeling unexpectedly overwhelmed, dealing with an emergency or everyday life. Some examples are: "Things are always working out for me," "I have a right to be seen and heard," or "The Universe is here to support me." For both my clients and myself, these phrases have a very calming effect.

6. Practice Good Yawning

Another technique I've been using myself and with my clients is to yawn. Yawning is a fast way to shift your energy and relax your brain. This allows you to put space between what your worries are and you. It helps declutter your brain, and it's quick, easy to do, and doesn't cost any money to implement. It's a great on-the-run tool to use throughout your day.

7. Use Tapping

Last, my favorite, is tapping, which we discussed in many places in this book. You can do some tapping on your own to help keep a negative emotion at bay. When you're ready for the big transformations, contact me and let's clear out the roots!

To keep grounded, create a routine that you implement daily. Which of these would you like to use?

GROUNDING ACTIVITIES

- tapping (visit www.KateBeeders.com/LearnToTap)
- mantra
- focus word
- celebrating
- gratitude
- journaling
- exercise
- eating healthy
- meditation

- » yoga
- » motivational videos
- » motivational audio
- » reading motivational materials
- » reading your vision statement
- » music
- » yawn

If you were going on a 10-mile hike for the first time, wouldn't it be a lot easier if you'd been eating healthy, were physically fit, and had taken other hikes previously, instead of showing up that day overweight, sluggish from too many doughnuts, and in a bad mood? You know which actions will get you the best results. Even though you might not be a dentist's daughter, you can still use preventive care in your daily life to keep you in your brilliance.

As you bring these supportive, grounding activities into your life, you're making yourself a priority. Taking these actions will help keep you grounded. You're putting that oxygen mask on yourself first. Nice job! Keep going!

Lessons in Brilliance

✦ Take personal responsibility for your life. You're an adult. Everything you have today is a result of the actions you took yesterday. If you want a different tomorrow, take personal responsibility and take a different action. For many, this is a big change.

✦ Create a daily routine using the choices from the "Grounding Activities" list. By implementing these actions on a regular basis, it will help you stay grounded no matter what happens. As a result, you'll end up making the best decisions for you instead of operating from a place of fear.

▶ **Don't Get Hijacked!** Continue to remember to put the oxygen mask on yourself first. Let go of any guilt you have around this. You won't be of service to anyone playing it small. With my clients, I've repeatedly seen how they not only made huge personal transformations as they shifted and changed, but they also became guiding lights and inspirations to others.

11

Be Brilliant

**"And the day came when the risk to
remain tight in a bud was more painful
than the risk it took to blossom."**
—*Elizabeth Appell*

When I first heard that quote in a transformational workshop, it propelled me on my entrepreneurial journey. I was making the decision of whether to stay in the corporate world or become an entrepreneur. This quote tugged at my heart so much that it brought tears to my eyes. I had to go forward. There was no other choice.

It's time for you to decide how important it is to have what you wrote in your vision statement.

How important is it? Take a moment and rate it again on a scale of zero to10. Zero being it doesn't matter and 10 that it must happen.

Now, ask yourself, what if you decide not to do anything differently, and as a result, nothing changes for you? What does that mean for you, your family, your relationships, your work, your community, and your legacy? Take a few minutes and journal how you would feel a year from now if you were in the same place as you are now.

At this point, you've got to decide. Go or Don't Go.

Either you will take action to build more success in your life or remain stuck. Will you choose to enter the Zone of Brilliance or to remain in your Comfort Zone? Only you can decide how important growth is for you.

Do you want to keep your money story or write a new one? The choice is yours. Go or Don't Go.

I hope you choose to be the brilliant person you are meant to be. By stepping into your brilliance, you become a beacon of light inspiring others to do the same

Go.

Gratitude

I am grateful to many people, without whom this book wouldn't have been possible.

To my sister, Jennifer Silbert, who has a gift of making everything possible, and my brother, Joel Beeders, who is on his own journey.

To my nieces and nephew, who are the future: Maddie, Coby, and Maya Beeders, and Ariel and Jillian Silbert. Thank you for the privilege of being your "favorite aunt." I enjoy that title more than you can imagine.

A special thank you to Sandra Anne Taylor, who initially taught me the Laws of Attraction and who continuously loves to remind me of how far I've come.

To Darren Hosier, who, perhaps on a whim, introduced me to "tapping," which has forever changed my life. And to Tim Fredrickson, who has been my friend through thick and thin and has always been there for me.

My Uncle Sol Saks wrote television shows and movies. His talent and creativity inspired me to write at a young age. He taught me that everyone wants to be an author, yet no one wants to put in the work to be a writer. Those words encouraged my efforts and strengthened my persistence to be an author and writer.

Success doesn't happen by itself; it takes a support system. To all the people who have continuously supported my dream, including my coaches, mentors, and team: Lynn Salatti, Michelle O'Neill, Cheryl Davey, and Michele Scism. To Carla Green, Marla Markman, and Allison Phillips for their expertise in getting this book written and published in a manner that makes me proud. There are too many others to name individually. I know in my heart that you know who you are. Thank you.

To my clients, it's because of you that I am here.

Best of all, to Cali Beeders, the very best girl in the whole wide world, who taught me about unconditional love and has shown me how big a heart I truly have.

Meet Kate Beeders

I'm an accidental entrepreneur. I started my business in 2010 after being laid off as a business development executive, and I was confident that I'd replace my multi-six-figure income (and then some) in no time.

Instead of big paydays, I was struggling to make ends meet. I was giving away my services because of an old money story that I wasn't aware of.

I was determined to make my business work. As a smart, committed professional, I knew I needed to get help. So I hired two coaches—one for marketing and the other for mindset—as no one had the level of expertise in both that I was looking for. They helped me learn how to handle my mindset, marketing, and money.

Quickly, I started making money. Then people started asking me to teach them what I was doing—and the Money Acceleration System™ was born.

The Money Acceleration System™ helps self-employed professionals, entrepreneurs, and corporate professionals tap into their Zone of Brilliance and make the money that matches their expertise.

Now, I'm no longer struggling, and I get to share my proven methods on stages across North America. I've been featured as a guest in telesummits with half a million participants, co-written a best-selling book, and even walked the red carpet in Hollywood.

Most important, I've helped thousands of people just like you go from stuck to successful with my focus on results. Plus, I'm from

Boston, so I give it to you straight and help you reach your vision. I'll tell you what you need to hear, not what you want to hear.

If you're ready to step into your brilliance and get big results, I can help. Contact my team at Info@KateBeeders.com.

Made in United States
North Haven, CT
06 April 2022

17973794R00071